Preaching In and Out of Season

Preaching
In and Out of Season

Edited by
Thomas G. Long
and
Neely Dixon McCarter

Westminster/John Knox Press
Louisville, Kentucky

Book design by Gene Harris

First edition

Published by Westminster/John Knox Press
Louisville, Kentucky

PRINTED IN THE UNITED STATES OF AMERICA
9 8 7 6 5 4 3 2 1

Library of Congress Cataloging-in-Publication Data

Preaching in and out of season / edited by Thomas G. Long and
   Neely Dixon McCarter. — 1st ed.
      p.   cm.
Includes bibliographical references.
ISBN 0-664-25149-8

1. Preaching.   I. Long, Thomas G., 1946–
II. McCarter, Neely Dixon, 1929–
BV4211.P737 1990
251—dc20   90-33573
                                                                    CIP

For Wade P. Huie, Jr.,

who, throughout his ministry,

has helped so many find the words

to speak the Word

Contents

Preface

The purpose of this book is to assist parish pastors with the demandingly regular task of preaching. Many preachers follow one of the lectionaries with their broad outlines of the Christian year. The editors in general affirm this practice, but we are conscious that even lectionary-based preachers must take into account other "calendars": namely, those occasions generated by the recurring program emphases of the church and by the holidays observed in our general culture.

Thus, Thanksgiving, family and marriage, race relations, ecumenical concerns, and the like are a part of every preacher's agenda. This book brings to such special days and events theological and biblical insights for the preacher.

It is therefore fitting that the volume is dedicated to Wade P. Huie, Jr., Peter Marshall Professor of Homiletics since 1957 at Columbia Theological Seminary, Decatur, Georgia. For more than thirty years, Professor Huie has devoted his life to the task of helping persons become preachers. This has usually meant taking "raw material"—that is, persons who have never thought much about preaching—and helping them become devoted servants of the Word without simultaneously developing messianic complexes. It has also meant working patiently with others who have a very clear definition of what they think preaching is all about and disabusing them of false notions and bad habits while helping them capture the real joy of proclaiming the good news.

Wade Huie uniquely embodies his discipline. For example, he has used his sabbatical leaves to share in the world mission of the church and to learn about preaching from Christians in Africa, Korea, and Jamaica as well as to share with preachers in these countries insights of his own. He has over these many years preached "in and out of season" across the face of this country and consequently has been called to numerous significant pulpits. He is a master of his art.

As a teacher of preaching, Wade Huie has struggled both with persons who believed quoting the Bible made their sermon "biblical" and with preachers who wanted to talk about interesting issues without concern for the biblical witness. He has helped many understand that one cannot appropriate the biblical message without also having a theological perspective, whether recognized or not. Thus there has been in his work a concern for the use of scholarly biblical and theological resources; a concern for the personal, even the psychological understanding of persons without psychologizing either the text or all of life's events; a concern for the world, not only the "secular" reality in which we live but especially the ecumenical oneness that is the church. Freshness and imagination, passion and conviction permeate "Huie-type" preaching.

Professor Huie's influence on the field of homiletics is symbolized by his election to the presidency of the Academy of Homiletics in 1979. Far more significant has been his ability to convince colleagues on theological faculties of the importance of preaching in the theological curriculum. He has managed to involve many colleagues from a variety of disciplines in the school's task of teaching preaching. Homiletics becomes an occasion when the components of curriculum come together.

This perhaps accounts for why so many of the contributors to this book are either former colleagues of Wade's, former students who learned to love preaching while working with him, or professors at other theological schools who have been influenced by him.

Wade is known to all of us not only as a preacher but also as a devoted husband, a patient and loving father, and a friend whom we can trust. His impact as a person on other people has

changed lives, prompted growth, and generated more encouragement than any of us can calculate.

All of us join therefore in dedicating this volume to Wade
P. Huie, Jr., with deep appreciation and affection.

Thomas G. Long   Neely Dixon McCarter
Princeton Theological Seminary   *Pacific School of Religion*
Princeton, New Jersey   *Berkeley, California*

Introduction:
The Three Calendars
of Preaching

Every pastor of a congregation is aware of the paradox of preaching. On the one hand, preaching is a demanding, urgent, and crucial activity. The pulpit is the central place where the vision of the Christian faith finds expression, and what happens in preaching radiates to all other areas of the church's life and mission: education, service, witness, and fellowship. Faithful preaching can enliven a congregation and profoundly shape its character. Incompetent preaching can drain a congregation's strength and trivialize its ministry.

On the other hand, though, a single sermon is a small and frail thing. It is a scaffolding seemingly too shaky to bear the weight of preaching's importance. Although dramatic responses have sometimes resulted from one sermon, most of the time one Sunday's sermon is but a trimming of the sails, a word among many words.

The truth is that sermons are cumulative in their power and effect. Generally it is not this Sunday's sermon, or that one, that dramatically shapes the life of the faithful community, but rather the gradual process of preaching week in and week out. Preachers stand Sunday after Sunday before congregations of people whom they are called to love and to nurture, and they preach. They preach not the whole gospel—what sermon could contain it?—but this or that part of the gospel for this day, for these people, and in this place. Slowly the rhythms are established, the grooves are cut, and the larger shape of the whole gospel appears.

One implication of this gradual and cumulative impact of preaching is that effective preaching must be planned. Preachers must think beyond the demands of next Sunday and toward the greater preaching pattern of which next week's sermon is but a single part. The full range of the gospel must be heard, but it cannot be heard in a day. The note sounded in one sermon must blend with other sermons to form the harmonies called forth by the fullness of the Christian faith.

Traditionally preachers have employed the Christian year as one valuable resource for planning their preaching. The sequence of seasons and festivals, each with its particular themes and special issues, serves as a comprehensive menu for the diet of preaching. Preachers who are pastors of congregations know, however, that they cannot respond only to the calendar of the Christian year. Two other calendars beckon them as well: the secular calendar and the program calendar of local and denominational emphases.

The secular calendar consists of those days and seasons by which the larger culture measures time, such as national holidays, the beginning and ending of public school, the vacation season, New Year's Day, and the like. Although it is sometimes fashionable in church circles to regard this calendar with disdain as an impure intrusion into the holier cycles of time, the fact of the matter is that people in the pews are significantly shaped by this calendar. Preaching that seeks to engage the world in which we live must address the real forces at work on people's lives or risk abstraction and irrelevance. If society interrupts the passage of time to rest, to remember, to play, to give thanks, to recognize, to honor, or to start again, Christian faith has a word to speak on those occasions. This word may be one of confirmation. It may be one of critique. It may be both. But there is a word to speak. If the forces at work in our culture are able to persuade the whole society to mark one day or season in the year as Thanksgiving Day, Super Bowl Sunday, Labor Day, spring break, or so-many-shopping-days-until-Christmas, the Christian community must discern what is at stake in this and respond.

The program calendar of the church is composed of those occasions and themes of ongoing importance to a local church or to its denomination, including such times as Race Relations Sunday, stewardship season, theological education Sunday, witness season, Peace Sunday, and the like. Such programmatic emphases always risk turning worship into a utilitarian event, a support for a series of good and noble causes, but in the best sense such occasions bring the commitments of the Christian community into sharper focus.

This book intends to be a resource for preachers who must plan their preaching not only according to the church year but also in response to the other two calendars. Many resources are available to assist the preacher in creating sermons in accord with the church year, most of them lectionary-based materials. But what of the preacher who wishes to engage in solid biblical and theological preaching in stewardship season or on the Sunday before Labor Day? It is to this need that the chapters in this book are addressed.

Each chapter in this book treats a major theme rather than a particular occasion or season. The reason for this is that each of these themes is pertinent on more than one occasion during the year. For example, David Buttrick's "Preaching About the Family—The Candor and Concern of Biblical Faith" addresses issues that are of obvious concern on days such as Mother's Day or Father's Day, but it is also a resource at other times, such as Christian Education Sunday, homecomings, weddings. Again, Joanna Adams's "Preaching About Church and Nation—Serving the God of All Nations" will provide help to the preacher for sermons not only on the Sunday closest to the Fourth of July and other national holidays but also in seasons of emphasis on peacemaking.

In providing theological and biblical reflection upon these ongoing concerns of the Christian church, we hoped that the week-in and week-out task of preaching may become more insightful, that the cumulative impact of the pulpit will become more effective, and that working preachers will find welcome support for the demanding task of preaching "in and out of season."

1

Preaching About Race Relations—
The Hope of Reconciliation

Richard Lischer

When Martin Luther King, Jr., characterized eleven o'clock on Sunday morning as the "most segregated hour of Christian America," he was quoting a saying that had already become proverbial.[1] The religious history of the races in the United States has been one of progressive separation. The eviction of Richard Allen and Absalom Jones from St. George's Methodist Episcopal Church in Philadelphia in 1787 formally marked the beginning of the black church in America. From that day forward, the partnership of blacks and whites in worship, which was common in many areas of the country and which would never entirely cease, became the exception to the rule. In the great revivals and camp meetings of the eighteenth and early nineteenth centuries, blacks were attracted to the emotional expression of Baptist and Methodist Christianity and in turn influenced these with call-and-response patterns inherited from Africa.[2] Blacks and whites sang together:

> Hold up the Baptist finger,
> Hold up the Baptist hand,
> When I get in the Heavens,
> Going a-join the Baptist Band.[3]

Yet, for African Americans, the new religious cosmos rested upon ironic foundations. The language of Christian piety and rituals of worship used by whites and blacks alike were attended by social conditions that made a travesty of their origi-

nal intent. The action on stage did not match the script, and
the longer it went on the more glaring was the discrepancy.
Blacks were converted to the religion of *koinōnia* by churches
that gradually excluded them from membership. The gospel
of freedom foundered on the shoals of real enslavement.

The original Christian impulse was to baptize the heathen
and to set them free. This was the Baptist and Methodist
agenda. On the Eastern shore the Methodist Francis Asbury,
accompanied by the famous preacher Black Harry, came
preaching a gospel of manumission and was greeted by slaves
as a white Moses. But by the beginning of the nineteenth
century, the plantation owners had mastered the preachers,
and state legislatures up and down the coast, aware of the
obvious implications of making black people brothers and sisters in Christ, issued caveats to the effect that baptism does not
confer political freedom or social equality. White Christians
first worshiped with their slaves and other Negroes, then ban-
ished them to the balcony, and finally separated from them
into segregated congregations. By the second quarter of the
nineteenth century even the most egalitarian expression of
American Christianity, the camp meeting, was divided along
racial lines, with Negroes assigned places to sit behind the
speaker's stand.[4]

By its very existence the black church continues to witness
to "the Veil," as segregation was dubbed by W. E. B. Du Bois,
which divides not only the social and economic realm but the
spiritual as well.[5] "The problem of the twentieth century," he
said in 1900 (!), "is the problem of the color-line."[6] In the
1940s Swedish sociologist Gunnar Myrdal described the relation of the races as the "American dilemma," "a dilemma
derived from the conflict between the high-sounding Christian
concepts embodied in the American creed as compared to the
way Americans really behaved."[7]

Despite enormous political changes effected by the civil
rights movement of the 1960s, the American dilemma continues. In matters of government, housing, and employment,
laws have been enacted to ensure some semblance of equality
of opportunity, though these laws, under the constant pressure of erosion, have had little impact on the overall economic

health of blacks in America. In spheres less amenable to legislation, such as social mores, patterns of interpersonal association, friendship, and organized religion, Du Bois's assessment of the "color-line" applies to our own day with its new wave of racial antagonisms. The problem of race relations in America is not one topic among many to be addressed in the pulpit, but *the* dilemma that has haunted American life from the beginning. It is the one issue on which the majority of white churches have most glaringly failed to transcend the sins of their culture. King was right when he said, "How often the church has been an echo rather than a voice, a tail light behind the Supreme Court and other secular agencies, rather than a headlight guiding men progressively and decisively to higher levels of understanding."[8]

The key to effective preaching on race relations, then, is the preacher's awareness of the problem's history and continuing significance. Rather than intellectualizing it as one problem among many, the preacher must recognize racism as the polluted atmosphere in which Christians and other Americans have been trying to breathe. The preacher does not address so comprehensive a sin with any one text but, as the German bishop Martin Niemöller said in another generation of the Christian responsibility toward Jews, it is in every text.

The weight of history is so great, and the problems of separation, distrust, and inequality of resources so all-pervasive, the preacher must know that words alone will not effect healing. The pulpit has failed too many times. In the nineteenth century, for every Henry Ward Beecher or Theodore Parker there were innumerable preachers who justified slavery on the basis of Holy Writ. In this century, for every white preacher who took a prophetic stance on the racial crisis there were twenty-five who preached sermons entitled "Why Integration Is Unchristian!" or "God the Original Segregationist."[9] For every activist in the black church there were far too many preachers who, as King often complained, limited Christianity to salvation over yonder.

While there will always be a place for the prophetic word that gets the preacher fired, today the word of healing and justice must arise from the prophetic congregation whose ongoing life and efforts are aimed at reconciliation. This will not be the congregation that has uncritically accepted the theory of "homogeneous units" as a means to church growth but rather one that is willing to sacrifice market appeal in order to exemplify the body of Christ. Black and white congregations in the same community or across the world may form partnerships in ministry and mutual encouragement. Sister congregations within the community may share social projects, sponsor interracial breakfasts, engage in regular pulpit exchange, and, in general, keep their antennae out for issues that polarize the community. In our city a black and a white Baptist congregation have formed a joint social ministry committee. Many communions have set aside a Sunday in February as Race Relations Sunday, but this has been widely supplanted by the churches' observance of the birthday of Martin Luther King, Jr., in January. An annual race-relations message given on an appointed day, however laudable its aims, will achieve less than preaching that is perennially sensitive to the American dilemma.

Theological Resources

In the context of mutual ministry the resources of doctrine and scripture offer a wealth of possibilities for preaching. The most powerful impetus to justice and reconciliation lies in what Amos Wilder called "essential sanctions": that is, commands that are grounded in the nature of God, God's activity, and the essence of the gospel.[10] "You, therefore, must be perfect," Jesus says, "as your heavenly Father is perfect" (Matt. 5:48). "For as many of you as were baptized into Christ have put on Christ. There is neither Jew nor Greek . . . ; for you are all one in Christ Jesus" (Gal. 3:27–28). And, again, Paul: "Only let your manner of life be worthy of the gospel of Christ" (Phil. 1:27a). These citations are not proof texts for use in sermons but are indicative of an approach to preaching on controversial subjects that does not rely on any one verse of scripture or on scriptural "data" that are not organically connected to the nature of God and the great themes of redemption in the Bible. Christianity inherited the entire Old Testament, including the lore on the children of Noah—Shem, Ham, and Japheth—and other texts that slaveholders and segregationists have quoted against racial equality. ("Our text plainly declares that by these three 'were the nations *divided* in the earth after the flood.' "[11]) But in service to its own proclamation, Christianity appropriated key metaphors—exodus, creation, sacrifice, law—and fleshed these out in terms of redemption, adoption, liberation, new creation, peace, reconciliation, and justification by faith. These are the essential sanctions, the building blocks, for any proclamation on the relation of the races. The preacher is always tempted to "improve" on these by relying on common sense, self-interest, psychology, or the politics of liberalism as substitute materials for the message. But when the preacher builds on an evangelical foundation, one that is rooted in the good news itself, he or she will articulate a word that is distinctly Christian, distinctively biblical.

The great danger in substitute approaches is moralism. Moralism has learned its lessons well from the Enlightenment on the virtue of brotherhood (and sisterhood), the inviolability of the individual, and the sanctity of freedom. It establishes these as goals for the congregation without relating them to essential sanctions in the nature of God and the gospel and without demonstrating how God-in-Jesus creates reconciliation and justice on a level that transcends the best of our moral ideals. Moralism, then, sets goals but does not provide the resources for attaining them. It does not tell to whom Christians may turn for empowerment toward reconciliation in race relations.

Moralism disregards the eschatological character of the Christian message. It grounds its admonitions in moral or religious ideals rather than in the new reality that has been unloosed among us in the ministry, death, and resurrection of Jesus. Martin Luther King, Jr., was particularly adept at urging racial justice, not because it represents a morally superior choice for any individual to make but because God's intervention in the suffering of the oppressed has redirected the world's history toward a new outcome.

The preaching of peace in racially divided communities, where Italians and Hispanics, or blacks and Jews, or Native Americans and Anglos live in daily tension with one another, should not be based on some historical or religious ideal of unity. To suppose that the church ever enjoyed perfect unity, even in the New Testament era, is to create an unreal world and false expectations. The proclamation of shalom among the races is rooted in an eschatological, not ideal, understanding of the Christian faith. Christians are a pilgrim people on the move toward the final and full disclosure of their identity as the people of God. We work for peace, reconciliation, and justice not because we have seen these ideals in some locatable past, or because they have a separate existence in a philosopher's heaven, but because we know by faith that they lie ahead. "Beloved, . . . it does not yet appear what we shall be" (1 John 3:2).

How do Christians know they are journeying toward peace and not ultimate fragmentation? Because the character of the end has already been revealed in the event of Jesus Christ. We do not make war on our fellow human beings, not because it is in our interest not to do so or because it violates established civil contracts, but because hatred has no place in the new reality that has already dawned and toward which we struggle.

The eschatological perspective need not entail otherworldly preaching. Black preaching about heaven or glory has been stereotyped as escapist by critics who did not fully appreciate the constraints on the black pulpit. The African-American preacher could sustain his people with a message of their inestimable dignity and their heavenly destiny. He (or in rare cases, she) could tell a Bible story and situate the hearers in the story in such a way that controversial and dangerous assertions would be unnecessary. But the preacher could not make a frontal assault on the sins of oppression without endangering the congregation and the ministry.[12] In this context, the chant of a contemporary black preacher—

> Let me lift the cur-tain of the fu-ture
> And show you a-bout my peo-ple.
> They may suf-fer down here,
> But I got a bet-ter place on the oth-er side.
> . . . Just hold on[13]—

is more eschatological than otherworldly in its hope in God's future. When the black preacher reaches the sermon's climax and begins to cross over the Jordan to the other side, the congregation is crossing over with him. Together, in the context of praise, prayer, and ecstasy, they both arrive, in a moment that may nourish a day or an entire week, at a place where all suffering has ceased and joy reigns. Far from being the opium of the people or a temporary escape from social or economic oppression, the sermon climax serves a subtler, more dialectical purpose. Those who criticize it as mere escape valve do not reckon with the symbol's power to actualize the thing it symbolizes. To experience the day of peace, justice, or triumph in the timelessness of worship will hasten the coming of that day in history. The ritualized cry for deliverance provides the form, if not the substance, of things to come. When a simple Macon County preacher in a sermon about Joseph chants his vision of the future, "And I *dream, chillun,* "[14] the *dream* unlocks his congregation's hopes for a better life no less than when Martin Luther King, Jr., moved his "congregation" toward justice with the same symbol.

Any number of the church's doctrines serve the cause of reconciliation among the races. The doctrines of creation, reconciliation, liberation, the image of God, the church (one, holy, catholic, and apostolic)—all rest on God's action in history, and all participate in the eschatological hope. The image of God, for example, refers not only to the rationality and goodness of Adam but to the perfection of that shattered image in Christ. If we cannot yet see our perfected image of unity, we can at least be assured that we are (or are meant to be) moving toward it.

Not every announcement of the essential sanctions—those rooted in God and the gospel message—is greeted with acceptance. What seems so obvious to preachers may not be clear to the congregation. Decades ago when angry parents were protesting the integration of an elementary school in New Orleans, a lone priest stood in the street in front of the mob and held before it a crucifix. That symbolic-prophetic action was to clarify the connection between the at-one-ment effected on the cross and the potential for reconciliation among people of different races. The mob did not see the connection.

While it is best that the prophetic word arise from the midst of a prophetic congregation that understands its own mission and enjoys partnership with Christians of another race, it will not always happen that way. While it is to be hoped that the "routine" activities of any congregation, such as baptism, Eucharist, and preaching, will automatically forge a connection between Christian revelation and social divisions, those connections are almost never made without conflict in the congregation. When the plowing of the field by means of education and consensus appears to have failed, the preacher is left with his or her own voice and the daunting responsibility of prophetic utterance.

Without relinquishing the sensitivity that characterizes pastoral leadership or the humility that reflects on the many ways the preacher is implicated in the sins of the culture, the prophetic preacher follows a fourfold movement:

1. He or she sketches the vision of justice or peace (and its ancient perversions) as it is outlined in scripture.

2. Next the preacher names the public evil and notes its manifestations in the midst of the congregation.

3. He or she then announces God's interruption of the cycle of sin in the event of Jesus Christ.

4. Finally, the preacher imagines for the congregation an alternate vision of a new way for the people of God.[15]

An Example Text

In a sermon on Ephesians 2:11–22, the preacher might teach the congregation that God's act in the cross of Christ removed the distinctions between Jew and Gentile, circumcision and uncircumcision, and made it possible for a far-off people to be included in an exclusive covenant. That reconciliation did not merely occur in the mind of God; it was meant to affect alienated people and races of every generation. The evil of racism, especially when it is harbored among Christians, is a way of rebuilding the wall of separation. Whenever social and political life is intentionally separated from the life of the Spirit, we have a clue that walls are being rebuilt. In this step it is important to avoid pointing the finger away from us toward the evils of apartheid, racism, intolerance "out there" in such a way that the congregation itself is exonerated. The preacher must speak to *our* tendency to characterize those of a different race or ethnic group as the stranger, the other, when in fact we were all once "separated," "alienated," and estranged from the divine covenant. Racism that declares the neighbor to be "other" is nothing less than a reversion to the pre-Christian existence of those who are *atheoi* ("without God," v. 12). "But now," the preacher continues, we have been brought near, not only to God but to one another. "For he [Christ] is our peace" (v. 14).

An exposition of that peace not only clears out the underbrush of false notions of peace but also recognizes the ambiguities that stalk the relationship of the races in America. Peace is coherence in the midst of trouble. It is not the solution but the principle by which all solutions will be found. The peace of God means freedom. Peace is the secure platform of our reconciliation through Jesus Christ that makes us all brothers and sisters. From such a platform we are now free to launch every fallible, experimental, and dangerous probe toward the realization of our unity in a society that is hostile to such efforts.

What might that unity look like? The author of Ephesians pictures it as a house built on God and filled with the Spirit. What might such a world-house look like in South Africa, or in rural North Carolina, where, in certain crossroads counties, Anglos, African Americans, and Native Americans encounter sojourning Mexicans? What does this Spirit-filled house look like in our parish, where resistance to a proposed day-care center for the elderly emerged from a not-so-hidden racial agenda? Only the preacher can imagine for the congregation the vision of people of all colors and cultural estates gathering around the table, *our* table, for the feast of the kingdom. Here the imagination of Martin Luther King, Jr., provides a model for a new generation of preachers striving to be true to their pastoral-prophetic vocation. "My people, my people, listen!" he cried in the conclusion of his Nobel prize acceptance speech. "The battle is in our hands."[16]

Notes

1. Martin Luther King, Jr., "Desirability of Being Maladjusted" (unpublished manuscript, January 1958, in the Archives of the Martin Luther King, Jr., Center for Nonviolent Social Change). The reference to 11 A.M. on Sunday as the most segregated hour comes from Liston Pope, *The Kingdom Beyond Caste* (New York: Friendship Press, 1957), p. 105.

2. Mechal Sobel, *Trabelin' On: The Slave Journey to an Afro-Baptist Faith* (Westport, Conn.: Greenwood Press, 1979), pp. 3–21, 102–110.

3. *Songs of Zion* (Nashville: Abingdon Press, 1981), no. 163.

4. Sobel, *Trabelin' On,* p. 98.

5. W. E. B. Du Bois, *The Souls of Black Folk,* in *Three Negro Classics* (1903 ed.; reprint New York: Avon Books, 1965), p. 214.

6. Ibid., p. 221.

7. See C. Eric Lincoln, *Race, Religion, and the Continuing American Dilemma* (New York: Hill & Wang, 1984), p. xiv.

8. Martin Luther King, Jr., "A Challenge to the Churches and Synagogues" (Holograph, n.d., Special Collections of the Mugar Memorial Library, Boston University).

9. See Dewitte T. Holland and others, eds., *Preaching in American History: Selected Issues in the American Pulpit, 1630–1967* (Nashville: Abingdon Press, 1969), p. 382; and Dewitte T. Holland and others, eds., *Sermons in American History* (Nashville: Abingdon Press, 1971), pp. 513–522.

10. Amos N. Wilder, *Eschatology and Ethics in the Teaching of Jesus* (New York: Harper & Brothers, 1939), pp. 47 and 57ff. See Richard Lischer, "The Sermon on the Mount as Radical Pastoral Care," *Interpretation,* vol. 41, no. 1 (April 1987), pp. 162–166.

11. Carey Daniel, "God the Original Segregationist," in Holland, *Sermons,* p. 514.

12. Eugene D. Genovese, *Roll, Jordan, Roll: The World the Slaves Made* (New York: Vintage Books, 1972), pp. 272–273.

13. Quoted in Jon Michael Spencer, *Sacred Symphony: The Chanted Sermon of the Black Preacher* (New York: Greenwood Press, 1987), p. 114.

14. William Pipes, *Say Amen, Brother!* (New York: William-Frederick Press, 1951), p. 118.

15. See Walter Brueggemann, *The Prophetic Imagination* (Philadelphia: Fortress Press, 1978).

16. "Nobel Prize Acceptance Speech," *A Testament of Hope: The Essential Writings of Martin Luther King, Jr.*, ed. James Melvin Washington (San Francisco: Harper & Row, 1986), p. 229.

2

Preaching About the Family—
The Candor
and Concern of Biblical Faith

David Buttrick

These days, preachers do not preach much on the family. Though churches are often manic with family activity, and spacious family life centers are attached to parish buildings all over the nation, the pulpit seldom addresses family problems. Of course, some congregations still observe Children's Day, often painfully, as well as mawkish Mother's Day ("Now here's a rose for the oldest mother!") and, of late, some sort of fling for "dear old Dad." Other parishes have consolidated these Hallmark days, replacing them with a Festival of the Christian Home, which while curbing excess sentimentality may well increase tedium. Once-a-year liturgical acknowledgments are always less a confession of the church's conviction than a symptom of guilty neglect. In most mainline Protestant churches, we seldom preach on the family.

Of course, to be honest, most of us clergy types are not well prepared to do so. In Catholic seminaries there are any number of required courses on marriage and the family crammed into the requisite four-year M.Div. curriculum: courses that study the family in relation to theology, sacraments, moral theology, canon law, sexuality, and pastoral ministry. By contrast, the average Protestant seminary may list an occasional elective tucked away among courses on pastoral counseling. As a result, most Protestant preachers, though often parents themselves, have no developed theological understanding of family. When it comes to considering the abrasions and mysteries of family living, most congregations are left with back issues of the *Ladies' Home Journal*—or worse.

Our pulpit silence, however, is maintained in the face of obvious need; these days the family seems strangely troubled. Have not national news magazines chronicled the crisis of the American family? Many of the somber, looming issues that shadow our common lives relate directly to patterns of family life—juvenile suicide, teen pregnancies, crack in our school corridors. Nowadays families seem fragmented: Marriages founder with little more than a fifty-fifty shot at success.[1] One misguided Protestant denomination has even proposed a liturgical rite of divorce! Tentative live-in relationships are so common that etiquette books now devote paragraphs to the problem of how we are to address "significant others." Home life is deficient; the term "latchkey kid" has entered the vocabulary in recent years. Perhaps Day-Care Day will soon replace Mother's Day on free church liturgical calendars! So most of us are concerned; like the television networks, we are basically "for the family." Yet, though family life is strained and marriages often border on pathology, the pulpit is largely mute. We do not preach much on the family.

Biblical Faith and the Family: Candor

At the outset, candor: According to Christian faith, the family is *not* an ultimate. From the start, newborn Christian faith strained patterns of ancient family life.[2] Family securities were shaken when early apostles left home to go on the road with the gospel message; clearly, preaching the gospel took priority over familial responsibilities. Likewise, family hostilities were enlarged when all-agog converts left traditional patterns of Jewish family practice for life in upstart Christian communities. Were early Christians castigated for family neglect? Probably, for there are a number of snarly texts that pit faith against family in our Christian scriptures.

In Luke, young Jesus seems quite unconcerned for family cohesion when he remains in the temple to "be about my Father's business" (Luke 2:41–50). Later, in Mark, when Jesus' family members come chasing after him, he asks bluntly,

"Who are my mother and my brothers?" and casts his lot with a bedraggled crowd, gathered to hear him speak (Mark 3:31–35). There is also Jesus' sharp retort, "Leave the dead to bury their own dead," aimed at a man who pleaded for time to observe his father's funeral, a rejoinder that subverted the sacred notion of family ties (Matt. 8:21–22).[3] Perhaps the cutting words that are found in Matthew 10:34–37 reflect early conflict between faith and family:[4]

> Do not think that I have come to bring peace. . . . I have come to set a man against his father, and a daughter against her mother, and a daughter-in-law against her mother-in-law; and a man's foes will be those of his own household. He who loves father or mother more than me is not worthy of me; and he who loves son or daughter more than me is not worthy of me.

We need not expect to find these words scribbled in a Mother's Day card! In Christian scriptures only the blood of Christ is thicker than water; the family is emphatically *not* an ultimate.

Moreover, early Christian communities were obviously regarded as new families superseding all previous family loyalty. Were they not designated "households of God"?[5] Did not Christians address one another affectionately as "Sister" and "Brother"? They saw themselves as children of God, a new family on earth, adopted by God through the saving love of Jesus the Christ. Though nowadays we complain that the church ought to be like a family, first-century Christians reversed the logic: every family was called to be a minichurch—with Christian instruction like glad preaching and Christian family meals like small-scale Eucharists. In other words, family life took its clues from the character and the calling of the church, not vice versa. For Christians the community of faith has been the *primary* family in which we find our true brothers and sisters, mothers and fathers. Perhaps the much-preached word from the cross, "Woman, behold, your son" / "Behold, your mother," bears witness to just such a new way of claiming relationship in the primary loyalty of Christian community.[6] Birth does not determine family ties for Christian people; baptism incorporates us into a new "family." All of this adds up to the assertion that in Christian theology the so-called nuclear family—its needs, its unity, its shared life—can never be ultimate.

Actually a demoting of family life may be liberation in our age when advertising is pitched toward the insatiable demands of the young and toward the incorrigible, if guilty, compliance of parents; toy stores are big business these days! We are a society that compulsively, even relentlessly, buys for its children. Of course, at the same time, less than 2 percent of the federal budget is earmarked for education. So we have an anomaly: We Americans sop the advertised cravings of the young while, at the same time, denying them truly important gifts of mind and spirit. Our family life is pathological; we spend dollars but subvert love. Perhaps the only way we can escape the clutch of family compulsions is to acknowledge that the peace of the family, its cohesion and its well-being, is simply not *the* priority of Christian people. In America, many of our social institutions have been tarnished. The political structures we have espoused as "democracy" have been eroded by cash-down corruption. Our courts no longer seem to court the free access of the poor. Our churches have plunged into tedious games of competitive self-preservation. We are left with our families, and therefore we tend to overinvest ourselves in family affairs. Christian faith can be liberating, for Christian faith announces that there are more important callings in life than family membership.

Biblical Faith and the Family: Concern

On the other hand, family life is not shunted aside by the scriptures, particularly the Hebrew scriptures. Obviously concern for the family is built into the so-called Ten Commandments: We should not covet a neighbor's spouse; we should honor our parents![7] Just as obviously, the Bible approves constancy in marriage, care in raising children, and fine festive family pleasures such as partying together. Biblical images are scarcely stuffy: psalms celebrate joys of marriage (Psalms 127; 128), and even Ecclesiastes, filled with dour ironies, urges us to enjoy life in marriage (Eccl. 9:9). Moreover, the Bible pictures (instruction can be so tedious) profound patterns of family love again and again, involving parents and children as well as children and children. All in all, though the family is not an ultimate in scripture, it is celebrated as a good gift of God's creation.

Moreover, the Bible uses family images to bring out our true relationship with God. God is a husband to Israel (Hosea 1–3), and Israel is God's chosen bride (Isa. 50:1; 54:4–6; 62:5). God is a mother cleaving to her young (Isa. 49:15; 66:13). God is a parent, indeed *the* parent of earth's human children. Such metaphors cut both ways; they illumine the character of God but also call us to godly love in family life. Implicitly, the Bible urges familial devotion, saying, in effect, "You must be parents as God is a parent!"—no small responsibility. So every parent serves under the true parentage of God.

The idea of God as the true parent of us all is worth further consideration. If God is the ultimate parent of our children, we are called to both freedom and trust. We can regard our children as "charges" under God's ultimate parentage: Our children are not *our* children—the possessive pronoun is always inappropriate—they are God's children though under our temporary care. But if children are ultimately God's children, we are relieved of a terrifying burden; our children need not worship us, thank God, much less regard our word as law, truth, or perfect wisdom. We are sinners and, as parents, enmeshed in ambiguity. Together with our children we may seek God's will and, happily, rely on God's good mercy, which, fortunately, is both wonderful and generously wide.

A same understanding fills the sacrament of baptism. In baptism our children are adopted by God, as brothers and sisters of Jesus Christ: "See what love the Father has given us, that we should be called children of God" (1 John 3:1). Thus, baptized, our children stand before God as we do; they are our equals in God's sight. Therefore, family life might be described as slightly older children bringing up younger children, for God is after all the only true parent. Does such a model undercut what is usually labeled "parental authority"? Why yes, of course it does! There is no fixed authority in family life other than the mediated Word and Spirit of God. Family is a locus. In families, we can seek the Lord, enjoy the Lord, and live together in the grace of our Lord Jesus Christ.

Marriage and Divorce

The Bible regards marriage as a gift of God and is somewhat stuffy on the subject of divorce. Yet in society today divorce is increasingly accepted as a psychological necessity, while at the same time marriages have become strangely tentative. Though we ministers may tend to relegate discussion of divorce to personal counseling lest we distress divorced members in a Sunday morning congregation, our reluctance is possibly unwise. As a family of God, every congregation needs marriages strengthened these days, and every congregation needs to consider the awesome terrors of divorce. Obviously divorce was a problem for early Christian communities, as it was for the Jewish society in which Jesus lived.

The classical text usually studied is Mark 10:1–12, for it deals with both marriage and divorce. The pericope is a "controversy/pronouncement" story with a defined form.[8] Controversy stories feature a question asked of Jesus, a counterquestion in reply, and finally an epigrammatic pronouncement. The pattern can vary with a brace of question/counterquestion, with scripture cited, or even with a brief inserted parable. In Mark 10, there is a doubled question/counterquestion pattern.

The question "Is it lawful for a man to divorce his wife?" may reflect a later concern of the Markan community. At the time of Christ, divorce was legal and the only questions circled around grounds for divorce. Deuteronomy 24:1–4 clearly permitted divorce if a husband "found some indecency" in a wife. The question is: What exactly constituted an "indecency"? In Judaism, the issue was debated by Shammai, a conservative party that would permit divorce only on the narrow ground of adultery, and Hillel, a liberal party that would allow divorce on a broader basis. But in Mark the question is much more sweeping: "Is divorce lawful?"

The counterquestion is terse: "What did Moses command you?" One way or another, counterquestions posed by Jesus *always* seem to expose the mind-set of his questioners. Here his questioners are legalists who assume that the law permits divorce. These days many people, if queried on the moral status of divorce, would answer in a similar fashion: "Well, it's legal isn't it?" Appeal to the law of the land has become an all-American way to avoid moral issues. But Christian ethics cannot be based on political consensus. Jesus said, "You are the light of the world." Our righteousness as evangelical Christians must be demonstrably more than some democratic moral consensus.

Then Jesus adds to his counterquestion a sharp word, "For your hardness of heart." His comment strikes home; even in our souped-up psychological age, marriage controversies can harden into rocklike hostile positions that seem to make reconciliation difficult or even impossible. Bluntly, sin is the necessity of divorce. Though clergy may be queasy about commenting on Jesus' tough realism, the words are not unhelpful. Most sensitive couples who have passed through agonies of divorce will acknowledge truth. Human sin is rather clearly involved in profound marital conflict, not to mention a hardening of hearts.

Suddenly the controversy form is expanded: Jesus quotes scripture and, what's more, appears to quote scripture against scripture, Genesis 2 over against Deuteronomy 24: "From the beginning of creation, 'God made them male and female.' For this reason a man shall leave his father and mother and be joined to his wife, and the two shall become one." Notice that in Genesis 2 the creation of sexual difference precedes the ordaining of marriage. But notice also that sexual difference is the basis of partnership—by a mathematics of love, two can become one! They become one through sexual coupling; there is no docetism of flesh here. We "know" one another sexually, and then, in the grace of justifying love, embrace such knowledge in a covenant of marriage. There is a profound, quite earthy theology of marriage implied in the citation from Genesis.

Finally, the pericope concludes with an epigrammatic exclamation: "What God has joined, let not a man rip apart."[9] The important thing for preachers to recognize is that the form of the pronouncement is epigrammatic; the words are *not* apodictic. None of the controversy/pronouncement stories ends up in law. Rather, the words are a free gesture toward the purposes of God. Although congregations (and ministers) may crave some clear-cut, fixed rule to live by, such is not found in

Mark 10:9. The question raised at the outset, "Is divorce law-ful?," is not answered but transformed; we must live in an awareness of God's good purpose for our lives and, within God's purpose, work out our salvation together.

Now, what about verses 10–12? They seem to be tacked on to the pericope, and they are. Clearly they refer to a somewhat different social setting, for they acknowledge a wife's discard-ing of a husband, which was not legally possible in Palestine during the time of Christ. Whenever Mark tacks on a private conversation with disciples ("In the house the disciples asked him again about this matter"), we usually encounter an inter-pretation that probably evolved in the community.[10] Here we do get a legal form: "Whoever divorces his wife and marries another, commits adultery against her; and if she divorces her husband and marries another, she commits adultery." Strong words indeed!

If we compare the Markan injunction with the same material in Matthew, we notice differences. Likewise, if we line up Mark and Matthew with the extended discussion of marriage and divorce in 1 Corinthians 7, we find still another position and a quite different style. Why the differences? Various Christian communities, all confronted by the same sweeping purposes of God, sought ground rules to guide their members. There-fore we cannot find any fixed rule handed down chipped in stone for contemporary Christians. What we find is a calling. In our churches today we must seek to shape our own pro-nouncements, guiding members in matters of marriage and divorce. The issues cannot be resolved within a therapeutic model alone. Instead, congregations must consider ethics and frame their understandings of both marriage and divorce in view of the judgment and mercy of Christ. What we must not do is to abdicate theological thinking either to the law of the state or to *Psychology Today*!

Social Roles and the Problem of Analogy

As we have seen, marriage is implied in the creation of female and male.[11] But in both the Hebrew and the Christian scrip-tures, marriage is also informed by analogy—marriage should enact God's covenant love for Israel and, in Christian communities, embody Christ's love for the church, his bride. The analogies might work well if they did not tend to express social sexism. Because the church is a servant people, must wives serve their husbands obediently? Or, because Israel was given commandments for the fulfilling of God's covenant purpose, must wives live by the commands of their godlike husbands? Clearly a host of texts that work from such familiar analogies have been perversely preached through the centuries by pulpits tacitly dedicated to male domination. Yet there are many passages in the Bible that put forth the analogies and, often, with particular reference to marriage. Can a more modern society simply skip the texts? If the contemporary mind can edit scripture without restraint, our Bibles could be reduced to little more than pamphlets!

There seems to be less of a problem with Genesis, as long as Genesis 2 and 3 are informed by the great text in Genesis 1: "So God created humanity in God's image; male and female [God] created them."[12] In spite of the often used male pronouns for God, the text does acknowledge that *both* female and male are in the "image of God" and that, in partnership, they *both* share the management of earth. Even the story of the shaping of woman in Genesis 2 can be interpreted as the creation of equal partners from a dozing, androgenous earthling.[13] But texts that inform marriage on the basis of analogy—God and Israel, Christ and the church—do not easily yield to homiletic reinterpretation in spite of the fancy exegetical footwork done by liberated scholars. Nevertheless, we cannot responsibly chuck the texts; they are in our Bible and often featured in liturgical marriage rites.

In part, problems can be eased if preachers can (1) pack away sexual role stereotypes and (2) focus on the revealed character of Godlove. Obviously sermons in which wives are pictured as little "helpmates," friendly cocker spaniel types who lick their master's hands and roll over on command, are both offensive and outright unchristian. Christians understand scripture as "a lamp unto our feet," which means scripture casts a light *ahead* of itself, including ahead of its own contextual stereotypes. The Bible must always be grasped through its promises; it looks to a new aeon in which there are no socially deformed notions of male and female. Therefore preachers must interpret passages in the light of eschatological vision,[14] but they must also be tough theologians. While we tend to define God triumphantly in terms of sovereign absolutes, the Christian tradition holds up a cross. God is the God whose love is so radical that God will abdicate position and die for loved humanity. The important aspect of the analogies, then, is radical covenant love; self-giving love to the nth degree! The analogies do not define status or dependencies; rightly understood, the analogies call us all—husbands, wives, and children—to a radical self-giving from the freedom of our created identities. The cross must inform the patterns of analogy.

Children and Parents

Actually the Bible doesn't hand out much advice on what is sometimes called parenting—a painfully cute term. In the Hebrew scriptures, we get narratives that tell tales of family life with both tenderness and a terrible realism; the Bible knows that we can be very dangerous one to another, particularly in family life. But also we can read wise epigrams that have been packed into the book of Proverbs. The proverbs urge parents to correct their children, saying in effect, "Don't spare the rod," and conversely call children to honor their fathers and mothers by heeding parental instruction. In the Christian scriptures, patterns of family life are discussed in the so-called *Haustafeln* (household rules) that appear notably in Ephesians 5:21–6:9; Colossians 3:18–4:1; and 1 Peter 2:13–3:7. The *Haustafeln* are conventional advice on relationships such as between husband and wife, children and parents, workers and bosses. They are not a Christian invention, for we find similar household rules in Aristotle, Seneca, Plutarch, and particularly in Stoic writings. At first glance, advice in the *Haustafeln* seems as wildly exciting as a stitched sampler on a kitchen wall. But if we explore the sayings, we stumble on some surprisingly apt wisdom.

Typical family advice is found in Ephesians 6:1–4, where it follows the famous exposition of marriage that draws on the analogy of Christ and church:

[1]Children, obey your parents in the Lord, for this is right. [2]"Honor your father and mother" (this is the first commandment with a promise), [3]"that it may be well with you and that you may live long on the earth." [4]Fathers, do not provoke your children to anger, but bring them up in the discipline and instruction of the Lord.

Certain observations may be in order. Verse 1: Because the passage follows immediately upon the discussion of marriage, it shares in the same analogy. Family life must also be in the Spirit of Christ, whose self-giving love is normative for Christians. Verse 2: Though one of the Ten Commandments is quoted, it is here understood as a call to obey parents *in the Lord:* namely, with the deferential love and mercy of Christ. As we all know, parents are as sinstruck as anyone else! Verse 3: The author of Ephesians quotes the commandment not so much imposing its rigor as emphasizing its promise of well-being and longevity, incidentally a longevity that leads beyond the lives of parents. Verse 4: Parents have an awesome responsibility. They must reach beyond themselves and the conventional mores of their society; they must instruct with the teaching of Christ and discipline with the generous mercy of Christ which they themselves have so undeservedly received. They must guard themselves so as not to generate hostility; hostility like a closed circuit can charge family life with an angry energy that is unresolved by "getting it out."

The key phrase in the passage is obvious: "in the Lord." The phrase gathers the whole passage into Christian community. So the model of family life derives from the relationship of Christ to the church; Christ instructs by the word, Christ is present in sacramental feasting, Christ forgives in the formal absolution, Christ gives in offerings. To bring up our children *in the Lord* is to model our family life after our common life in the community of Christ. In Christian understanding, every family is to be a minichurch, living not for itself but for the wider kinship of the world. As parents we read the passage, grabbing at words like "obey," "discipline," "instruction," eager for authority. But in Ephesians the only authority is quite explicit: namely, the love of Christ who has lived and died for all of us poor sinners—parents and children alike!

Preaching on the Family

We do not preach much on the family. Why? Are we uneasy about the enterprise? If we are celibate priests, our sermons may seem somewhat odd to our well-married, wised-up parishioners. If we are married ministers, our family life may stand in silent contradiction to our words—preacher's kids have been known to be either painfully prim or genuine hellers! Or is there something intrinsically dull about family sermons? Perhaps. All too often family sermons turn into labored expositions of analogy or trivial good advice or, worse, homiletic excursions into pop psychology. How on earth can we preach on the family and be both interesting and profound?

Let's explore three homiletic ground rules.

1. Sermons on the family ought to be marked by a kind of honesty. Actually family life can be quite trying; tensions between husband and wife are scarcely pleasant, sex can be a demonstration of our brokenness, not to mention somewhat untidy, and children are frequently little terrorists who hold their parents hostage. While spontaneous family hoopla can delight, there are as many griefs in family life as giggling joys, and sometimes more. So our sermons should not put forth idealistic pictures of American family life as do TV sitcoms or, more demonically, TV commercials. The fact is, family life is as much a witness to our common sinfulness as anything else. (No wonder that ancient theologians brooding the mystery of marriage and the family framed the doctrine of original sin!) Therefore sermons on the family ought to be preached with a degree of wide-eyed realism that is informed by Christian understandings of the human demonic.

However, realism ought to inform our images of family well-being as well. All too often, sermons picture the "happy family" euphorically in pastel greeting-card shades. The joys we do have in family life have their own earthy style and peculiar character—perhaps because they happen as grace in the midst of brokenness. Actually, the true joys of family life happen in such a way as to transcend the determinate nature of the family. If a family party takes off into glad celebration, it exceeds

itself and gives some hint of an ultimate, eschatological celebration among God's new humanity. If love in marriage is
particularly splendid (king-sized beds are a helpful invention),
it can be a sign of the self-forgetful giving to which we are all
called by God. We get these hints and signs in the particularity
of our families—our broken, mismanaged, conflicted families—as gifts of grace.

Realism in preaching is hard work. We must gaze at our own
mnemonic images with a phenomenal eye for actualities to
describe. To do so we will have to banish the false images put
forth by social roles and social idealisms. Americans have ro-
mantic images not only of married love but of family life, and
romanticism is generally deceptive. On the other hand, what
we call realism is frequently blind to unseen patterns of do-
mestic grace. What may be required is hard, bright theological
vision.

2. Sermons on the family ought to be informed by eschatology.
When Jesus was asked about the status in resurrection of a
much-married woman, he observed that in God's new order
there would be no marriage. If no marriage, then in the realm
of the risen there will be no permanent family definitions.
Presumably, married life is a temporary "order of creation."[15]
And perhaps families are merely training camps for a wider
new humanity in which we will all love our neighbors as our
own.[16] All of which is to say that families are not an end in
themselves. In families, we are called to live beyond family.
The end of God's salvation will not be a perfect nuclear family,
sticky with the smell of sanctity, but a gleeful humanity living
exchanges of love up and down the glassy streets of the city
of God! So the family cannot be saved by faith, church attendance, prayer, psychological insight, or anything else; the family
is redeemed as it leads to life in God's wider family, a new
humanity.

3. Sermons on the family ought to speak beyond moralism.
While the book of Proverbs is well aged and wise, sermons that
come out sounding like strung-together proverbs can be impossible. We preachers are not very good at good advice, so

our sermons on the family should not feature ten easy rules for family living or bons mots to enhance family happiness. If we aim at helpful guidance, we will almost always become Polonius in the pulpit, given to windy pontificating. What Christian faith offers is not so much practical advice for family living as theological understanding—even if we preach from Proverbs. The only way to avoid trivia is to set the family in a theological framework of God's free covenant election of humanity and God's mysterious purpose: namely, redemption. The true textbook for family sermons is a story, a story begun in scripture but not yet concluded, the story of God and humanity through Jesus Christ the Lord.

So, let us confess our failures: We do not preach much on the family. And let us take a deep breath and risk resolve: We will speak of the family often, and always *in the Lord.*

Notes

1. Cited from U.S. Census Bureau figures by Elizabeth Achtemeier, *Preaching About Family Relationships* (Philadelphia: Westminster Press, 1987), p. 21.

2. Gerd Theissen, *Sociology of Early Palestinian Christianity* (Philadelphia: Fortress Press, 1977), pp. 11–12.

3. See the discussion of the saying in E. P. Sanders, *Jesus and Judaism* (Philadelphia: Fortress Press, 1985), pp. 252–255.

4. Rudolf Bultmann argues that the church "experienced the fulfillment of the prophecy in its own life." See Rudolf Bultmann, *The History of the Synoptic Tradition* (New York: Harper & Row, 1968), pp. 154–155.

5. For discussion of the image, see Paul S. Minear, *Images of the Church in the New Testament* (Philadelphia: Westminster Press, 1960), pp. 165–172. The word "household" is more extensive than our intimate definitions of family.

6. For discussion, see Rudolf Schnackenburg, *The Gospel According to St. John,* vol. 3 (New York: Crossroad Publishing Co., 1982), pp. 278–279.

7. See Walter Harrelson, *The Ten Commandments and Human Rights* (Philadelphia: Fortress Press, 1980), pp. 92–105, 122–133.

8. For a study of the "Controversy/Pronouncement Stories," see Arland J. Hultgren, *Jesus and His Adversaries* (Minneapolis: Augsburg Publishing House, 1979).

9. My translation brings out "*a* man," which is in the Greek, as well as the violence in "rip apart."

10. Ever since Bultmann (*History of the Synoptic Tradition*, pp. 132, 148), most scholars have agreed that Mark 10:11–12 reflects a later church regulation.

11. For a helpful if somewhat Barthian study, see Paul K. Jewett, *Man as Male and Female* (Grand Rapids: Wm. B. Eerdmans Publishing Co., 1975).

12. For a useful survey, see Adela Yarbro Collins, "An Inclusive Biblical Theology," *Theology Today*, vol. 34, no. 4 (January 1978), pp. 358–369.

13. Until woman is created in Genesis 2:22–23, the Hebrew "man" might better be translated "earthling" (*ha'adam*, literally "of the earth").

14. Biblical authority is "rooted not just in the past but in the anticipation of God's intended future." Letty M. Russell, *Household of Freedom: Authority in Feminist Theology* (Philadelphia: Westminster Press, 1987), p. 25.

15. I have always enjoyed John Calvin's blunt assessment of marriage: "Marriage is a good and holy ordinance of God; and farming, building, cobbling, and barbering are lawful ordinances of God." *Calvin: Institutes of the Christian Religion*, ed. John T. McNeill, tr. Ford Lewis Battles (Philadelphia: Westminster Press, 1960), p. 1481.

16. David Noel Freedman has argued convincingly that the injunction to "love our neighbors as our selves" is a misunderstanding of Leviticus 19:18. The commandment calls us to love neighbors as our "own": namely, our own kinfolk. See "The Hebrew Old Testament and the Minister Today," *Pittsburgh Perspective*, vol. 5, no. 1 (March 1964), pp. 9–14, 30.

3

Preaching About Church and Nation— Serving the God of All Nations

Joanna Adams

It was ten fifteen on a summer Sunday morning; the decade was the '80s; the date was July third. As was her custom, the pastor went into the church sanctuary to turn the pulpit Bible to the text for the day, check the microphone, and attend to a few other fussy little tasks that filled up the hour before worship started and served the very useful purpose of calming the pre-preaching jitters that usually set in around that time. The chairperson of the altar guild had gotten there ahead of her that day. She had already taken the American flag out of the flower room and had unfurled it beside the pulpit.

"What's the flag doing here?" the pastor asked. This was her first Independence Day Sunday in the parish since graduating from seminary.

"We always have the American flag on Independence Day Sunday," the altar guild chairperson patiently explained to her young pastor. "The people expect it."

And so they do. People come to church the Sunday before the Fourth of July (and on certain other Sundays as well, such as Memorial Day or the Sunday just prior to a national election) expecting the wall of separation between church and state to be temporarily taken down. They expect the church to speak to the social order of which they are a part. The pastor who is rightfully wary of the co-option of faith for the purposes of patriotism would nevertheless be well served to remember both religious and secular history.

43

Certainly, the Judeo-Christian tradition has encouraged people of faith to participate in public life as a part of their religious responsibility. The reasons for the encouragement have had more to do with providence than with patriotism. Our forebears in faith were aware of how easily love for country could come to occupy an equal or greater place of reverence in the human heart than love for God, but they also worshiped the one God whom they believed to be "above all and through all and in all." Thus politics and the public order, particularly in the Reformed tradition, have been viewed as areas of God's domain as surely as theology and ecclesiology.

In order to prepare to preach on the church and the nation, the preacher might find it helpful to review briefly the relationship between the Christian faith and the state as it has been historically interpreted in the United States.

The New World was settled by Protestants who came with the intention of establishing "a holy nation," "a city set on a hill," and "a working model for a godly society," and the Declaration of Independence referred to "Nature's God," "the Creator," and "the Supreme Judge of the World." By the time the last musket of the Revolutionary War had been fired, however, the already diverse inhabitants of the thirteen colonies were committed to ensuring religious freedom. Tolerance had become the watchword of the day in a land in which less than 7 percent of the people were church members. The illustrious Deist Thomas Jefferson reflected the prevalent attitude: "It does me no injury for my neighbor to say there are twenty gods, or no god. It neither picks my pocket nor breaks my leg."

Our forebears were not always in agreement as to where God's providential hand was leading them next, or that there was such a hand at all; Quakers and Congregationalists, Presbyterians and Episcopalians, Deists and Dissenters were often at odds. Out of this rich mix of American diversity emerged an unprecedented, peaceful solution to one of the most perplexing problems of human society throughout the ages: how church and state are to be related to each other. What was intended to be a permanent wall was erected between them. Religious tests for public office were expressly forbidden by the Constitution. No one religious group would receive special governmental favor over another. Denominations would be free to grow and flourish, as indeed they did, without having to depend on the goodwill or generosity of the state.

The framers of the original charters of our government had learned well a critically important lesson of history: Those civil authorities that claim to rule by divine right, that establish one religion to the exclusion of other religions, often do so at the expense of freedom—dissidents persecuted, divergent views outlawed.

For over two hundred years, the First Amendment has succeeded in protecting American citizens from government participation in religious life, but it never was intended—nor should it be interpreted—to mean "separation of religion from community or separation of the church from public life."[1] It has always been the responsibility of the faith community throughout the history of this nation to tell the truth about the ways of God to the nation and to be the intercessor for the nation before God. We preach on the subject of church and nation not only because the people expect it, and the calendar calls for it, but because faithfulness requires it.

Biblical and Theological Resources

Among the many relevant theological and biblical models that could illumine a pastor's treatment of the topic of church and nation, four seem particularly rich.

The faith community as the conscience of society. In biblical history, God is rarely seen sending emissaries to people in power with instructions to pat those political leaders on the back and give them a plaque for serving God's purposes in such splendid ways. God is more often seen sending prophets to speak confrontive, corrective truths to people in power. "The word of the LORD came to Elijah, in the third year, saying, 'Go, show yourself to Ahab'" (1 Kings 18:1). Amos assails Jeroboam. Jeremiah lambasts Jehoiakim. The effect of such truth-telling is sometimes fatal. In the Brief Statement of Faith of the Presbyterian Church (U.S.A.) is the statement, "Unjustly condemned for blasphemy and sedition, Jesus was crucified . . . for the sins of the world." Jesus had dared to challenge political power as well as the religious authorities, and for that, he died.

The Bible is full of instances in which God sends people of faith to tell the truth to people in power. Sometimes, however, God instructs the prophet to fuss at the faith community itself for not living up to its calling of telling the truth to people in power. Jeremiah's temple sermon (Jer. 7:1–15) is directed at a religious community that has, in fact, directed all its energies toward doing religious things and has allowed the nation to neglect justice and oppress the alien and shed the blood of the innocent. The prophet Ezekiel, when he sees disaster looming on Jerusalem's horizons, directs his harshest words not to the leaders of the government but to the leaders of the religious community who have chosen to remain silent in the face of injustice.[2] "My hand will be against the prophets who see delusive visions and who give lying divinations . . ., saying, 'Peace,' when there is no peace" (Ezek. 13:9–10).

To be faithful to its prophetic role is one of the greatest challenges faced by the faith community in any age. Societies much prefer chaplains who bless the status quo to prophets who question and challenge the way things are. Yet God has given the church to the society as the means by which God's will might be revealed. It is an inherent, God-given characteristic of the church that it be the means by which the decay that perpetually threatens any society in a fallen world is kept from doing its worst. "You are the salt of the earth," Jesus said (Matt. 5:13). Surely, that job description for Christ's church still stands.

The faith community as the community of freedom. "For freedom Christ has set us free," Paul writes; "stand fast therefore, and do not submit again to a yoke of slavery" (Gal. 5:1). The Christian in the United States is the beneficiary of two kinds of freedom—political freedom and freedom in Christ—and, while they are related (all political freedoms are derivatives of the freedom that comes from God), they are not synonymous. The preacher should be careful not to muddle the two. The ideal of political freedom and the guarantee of religious liberty are hallmarks of American democracy. Freedom from oppression, freedom for self-expression, freedom to pursue life, liberty, and happiness are all rights constitutionally guaranteed to American citizens. Our forebears made sure that the government would stay out of the business of the church and that the rights of the individual would be protected from any intrusion upon his or her inner conscience or on the outer practice of the faith.

The Bible does not speak of the sort of religious liberty we know today. The scriptures were written in cultures in which democracy was unknown, so it would be a historical mistake to infer that, when the Bible speaks of freedom, it means the kind of freedom Americans rightfully hold dear. And yet, who can deny that "the glorious liberty of the children of God" has had manifestations throughout history, especially in the United States, that neither Paul nor any other biblical writer could have imagined?[3]

The Bible does speak of freedom in Christ, which is still God's gracious gift to believers today. Freedom in Christ is not the result of any human ideal or endeavor; it is not realized through any social enterprise or granted by any political charter. It is a gift from God. It is not so much the freedom to do one's own thing without interference as it is the freedom for community—with God and with one another.

The faith community as the community of repentance. Over against the self-congratulatory optimism of much contemporary patriotism stands the sober realism of the Christian faith with regard to human sin. "The Christian doctrine of original sin, this unpleasant fact in which we get our noses rubbed on Sunday morning, is our gift to the body politic."[4] Scripture reveals a God who takes sin very seriously. Scripture declares that sin is the one universal characteristic of the human creature and of all the institutions, political and otherwise, that humans create: *All* have sinned and fallen short of the glory of God. Contemporary society cannot do without faith's understanding of the nature and extent of human sin; without it, politicians and the people who vote for them are left with the illusion that in the public sphere all motivations are altruistic. Certainly, most contemporary political rhetoric implies that such is the case.

In an age in which sackcloth and ashes are out of fashion, the preacher's greatest challenge is to remain faithful to the gospel of repentance. No nation is perfect or ever will be perfectly aligned with the purposes of God. To say that is true of *our* nation is not to be unpatriotic. It is to make faithfulness to the purposes of God possible. Whenever individuals or nations convince themselves that their goodness is what saves them, they are in peril. People and nations are saved only by the righteousness of God. The Christian understanding of repentance is faith's answer to that most dangerous and seductive of all sin—pride.

The faith community as the community that witnesses to the peace that comes from God. Often, preaching on peacemaking implies that people of faith are the ones who make peace and that, if we get lazy about it, there will not be any peace. Biblical faith attests to exactly the opposite. God makes peace. Indeed, the biblical witness is to the God in whom peace not only originates, but who is not going to be content until peace prevails everywhere. The days are coming, the prophet Micah promises, when God "shall judge between many peoples, and shall decide for strong nations afar off; and they shall beat their swords into plowshares, and their spears into pruning hooks; nation shall not lift up sword against nation, neither shall they learn war any more" (Micah 4:3).

It is intriguing to consider why Micah chose to use the expression, as the Revised Standard Version translates the Hebrew, "Neither shall they *learn* war any more." Perhaps it is that war is a learned behavior and that this idea of wanting to harm our enemy is a bad habit we human beings have gotten into, that God has always meant that peace was to prevail.

Another rich text for preaching on peace is the second chapter of Ephesians, especially verses 14–22. Paul writes to the church: Jesus Christ *is* our peace. Jesus Christ *has made* us one. Jesus Christ *has broken down* the dividing walls of hostility. Notice the tenses here: it has already happened; it is done; peace is made. The world doesn't know that, and the world won't know that unless the church does what God put the church in the world to do, which is to witness to and testify to the alreadiness of the reign of God.

Preaching on Church and Nation

Here are three strategies for preaching on church and nation themes.

1. Sometimes well-known texts can take on a new dimension when viewed through the thematic lens of church and nation. The story of the Good Samaritan (Luke 10:25–37) is a case in point. A new approach to this familiar story might be to ask, on Economic Justice Sunday or the Sunday closest to the Fourth of July, if the time has not perhaps come to do something about the bandits along the road to Jericho, about the social and economic forces that leave people beaten up and lying in the ditch of hunger and homelessness in our land of abundance. The Good Samaritan is a story full of surprises, but the surprises have become as familiar as a well-worn pair of bedroom slippers. Most people who sit in pews know by now that none of the original hearers would have expected the Samaritan to be the hero. Most people know that the priest and the Levite, the professional church people, don't do what the original hearers expected them to do. A way to reclaim the surprise with which the parable was originally received might be to make a fresh homiletical move. Based on the Samaritan's extraordinary showing of compassion for the man beaten and robbed and left lying in the ditch, could not the preacher invite the congregation to speculate about where the Samaritan was going after he left the inn?

Perhaps he was simply going on about his business, but considering his behavior in the story so far—his getting involved up to his elbows in response to the need of the one in the ditch—is it at least possible that when he left the inn he was headed on back to Jerusalem, to the place where public priorities are set, to see if something couldn't be done about those awful bandits on the road?

Augustine wrote centuries ago:

> We cannot wish that others be unhappy so that we may have a chance to show our mercy. You give bread to the poor, but it would be far better if none went hungry. Do away with misery and there will be no need for mercy.

Do away with the bandits, and people can travel to Jericho in safety.

In a society that seems itself to be stuck in a ditch of indifference, stuck somewhere between acknowledging that there are people who are suffering and deciding to do something about it, the story of the Good Samaritan invites preachers to tell God's people the familiar story of the Good Samaritan in a surprising way. It invites us to trust once again the power of the story to get the society of which people of faith are a part on its way to being human again.

2. I remember well the first time I stood in a pulpit and issued a declaration of pardon. I spoke with all the feeling I could muster those great and gracious words from Romans: "Who is in a position to condemn? Only Christ and Christ died for us—Christ rose for us."

I remember that just as I got out those words, the lips of a fellow on the front row parted, and he began to open his mouth. He continued to open his mouth until he had produced what surely was the widest yawn on record east of the Mississippi. It was such a long, luxurious yawn, I could have inventoried his fillings if I'd wanted to. It occurred to me that he was yawning because I was boring him—I wasn't telling him a thing he wasn't sure of already. He knew he was pardoned. "Your sins are forgiven!" I said.

I know that! he thought. You preachers tell me that every Sunday. You've convinced me that God is as congenial and easy to get along with as can be.

That is why, every now and then, God sends someone like Jeremiah to wake people up to the whole truth about God, the God who offers grace unconditionally, to be sure, but the God who also requires the righteousness that grace makes possible.

In the face of the great, yawning indifference of the people of Judah to the moral and ethical demands of faith, God hurled the prophet Jeremiah—dead to the world, the people were. It was not that they had forsaken the faith; they had done what was even worse in the eyes of God—they had diminished the faith. They had decided to treat the Ten Commandments as ten suggestions, obedience optional. They had deceived themselves into believing that saying religious words and singing religious songs and following religious rituals gave them license to do what they pleased.

Jeremiah loved the people of God too much to let them be what they had become, and so he preached God's truth to them—right in the gate of the house of the Lord (Jer. 7:1–15). The prophet was not called to tell people what they wanted to hear; the call was to stab them awake with the truth of God that always stands over against the half-truths and the untruths people of faith like to tell themselves.

To call God's people to repentance in any age is to take a great risk. There is a far greater risk, however, and that is to ignore the life-giving righteousness of God, without which God's people will surely perish, along with their illusions.

Who said it first, that when God created the world God tilted the world toward justice and righteousness and compassion? To live any other way is to live out of balance with the way things are, and it will just not work. Jeremiah knew it. You go after those fake gods, he said, to your own hurt. As pastors, shall we not try to prevent the hurt that is inevitable when any society ignores the ways of God?

3. Preaching on the theme of church and nation leads us to consider our most basic understanding of the nature of God. It invites us beyond geographical boundaries; it propels us beyond partisan politics, because whatever we say about our country and our church must be grounded in God's hope for the world. Our hope as people of faith can be nothing less than God's hope, and God's hope is for the shalom of the whole created order. Scripture, from Genesis to Revelation, witnesses to a God whose concern is constantly widening. The Old Testament reveals a God who claims not only Israel but all nations of the earth for God's gracious purposes. The New Testament ends with Revelation's version of the new heaven and the new earth, the salvation of the cosmos itself.

I am convinced that the church has no more important calling, as we come to the close of the twentieth century, than to keep pulling on the coattails of a world that has accepted the inevitability of war, and that resorts to violent solutions to so many of its problems, and say, "These are not the ways of God!" The world is badly misinformed about the ways of God and where the world is going: It will come to pass in the latter days, the prophet Micah promises, that God's way will reign.

Not the one with the most nuclear warheads, but the One with the most love will win in the end. The One with the most justice will win in the end. In the end, God is going to have God's way with this world.

In the movie *Full Metal Jacket*, a general says to a young soldier, "Son, we're going to have to keep our heads until this peace thing blows over."

To preach on peace is to remind God's people that this peace thing is not going to blow over, that the day is coming when "nation shall not lift up sword against nation, neither shall they learn war any more." It is to feel God's Spirit creating in your own spirit a renewed passion for peace.

May our pledge of allegiance and our preaching of the gospel on any Sunday of national significance serve the purposes of the God of all the nations.

Notes

1. Religious Liberty Report to the 200th General Assembly (1988) of the Presbyterian Church (U.S.A.), Advisory Council on Church and Society, 37.1166.

2. Walter Brueggemann, "Truth-Telling and Peacemaking," *Christian Century*, Nov. 30, 1988, p. 1096.

3. Religious Liberty Report, 37.1191.

4. William H. Willimon, "Repentance and Politics," *Journal for Preachers*, Pentecost 1989, p. 11.

4

Preaching About the Global Witness of the Church— Loving the World as God Loves It

Catherine Gunsalus González

The theme of "global witness" reflects the claim that the innermost character of the church is to be worldwide, not to be limited to a certain group or nation. By nature and by intention, by calling and by mission, the church is global. The church is not to be provincial. This is partly what we confess in the Nicene Creed, when we say we believe the "one holy catholic . . . church." The first of these words speaks of the unity of the church. "Holy" we can understand fairly readily. But what does it mean that the church is "catholic"? Often we use the term "catholic" as another way to express the unity of the church. In some sense it does, but the catholicity of the church, as expressed in the creed, points particularly to its character as universal, as global, the whole of which the local, particular congregation is a part. For the church to be catholic means that it is not tied to one culture, that it can be a part of every culture, even though it also judges every culture.

Yet our experience of the church is local. Our experience of the church is within a certain culture—with music and architecture that are familiar to us, with customs and issues that relate to us. To become a Christian is not to leave one's culture behind and join some Christian culture that has no earthly homeland, even though our faith may well make us exiles from some elements of our own society. The church needs to be at home in the various places where congregations gather. The incarnation itself points to the indigenous character of the church.

Both concepts are true: the church is global and it is local. To be global in our awareness does not mean to negate the character of the particular. To be catholic does not mean to be removed from the specifics of the local situation. But how do we keep these together? How do we—in the midst of the everyday life of a local congregation or of a national church—keep in our mind that there are other congregations in radically different cultures, other national churches facing very different situations, and that we are each equally "the church"? Even more, it is together that we are the church. Nor can our concern for the world be limited to those places in which there is a church. We are to be witnesses to the local congregation of that whole world for which God is concerned. Furthermore, how do we help the global church to be aware of the many local, particular congregations of which it is composed, and of the needs of particular places in the world, even if there is no church there?

Particularly for Protestants, in the nineteenth century and into the twentieth, the impulse to be in mission to the areas of the world in which the Christian faith was unknown brought an awareness of the global goal of the church to most local congregations in our country. Sometimes it was difficult both for the Christians who went in mission and for the new Christians to be clear what was the gospel that needed to become a part of this new culture, and what was the Western culture in which it was brought.

Now in the latter part of the twentieth century, with churches strong throughout the world and a part of a wide variety of cultures, we Christians in this country face a new challenge. Clearly, to be global still means to be in mission to the whole world. But our global awareness must take into account these new churches that are at home in their cultures. They are churches as authentically as we are. How do we witness globally with them and to them? How do we allow them to witness with and to us? How do we understand that these other churches are part of the givers of mission and not simply the recipients? How do we keep in our thoughts and our prayers, in our worship and our planning, the awareness of this catholic reality of the church and of the world to which we are called to be witnesses? How do we do this without ceasing to be local, related to the particular situation and society in which we find ourselves? We are called to witness locally to the global reality of which we are a part; we are also called to witness globally to the local reality of which we are a part.

Global Witness Through the Year

Throughout the church year there are several times at which this global reality can be pointed to quite readily and naturally. Let us go through the liturgical year in the sequence in which we experience it. The significance of the sacraments for global awareness and witness will be discussed at particular points within the church year.

Advent and Christmas. Throughout both the Advent and Christmas seasons, the coming of God into human history in the midst of the very specific, concrete cultural and social situation of ancient Israel points to the character of God's continued presence in the body of Christ which is the church. The church therefore also has to be related in depth to the place in which it finds itself, as an authentic act of incarnation. At the same time, the body of Christ is one, not many. Though related to many cultures, we remain one church.

Since this time of the church year is so filled with customs that are particular to the cultures in which the church has developed, these can be used to show how the season is celebrated around the world. This can be especially helpful with children and families. In addition, since the church often had to go through some long and painful periods of determining what of the culture was appropriately "baptized" by the church and what must be discarded or opposed as inappropriate for Christians, tracing this history in our own and other cultures could be very helpful in evaluating our present celebrations of the seasons. Where did holly and Christmas trees, Advent wreaths and Christmas stockings come from? How do we determine what of pre-Christian or secular culture can be authentically a means of relating the church to the surrounding society—an authentic incarnation—and what parts detract from the gospel itself and are an illegitimate acculturation? Can we benefit from how those in other cultures have carried out this task? Can Christians from other cultures be helpful in our evaluation of our own celebrations? Do they have celebrations that we might find useful? As our own communities become more ethnically pluralistic, we may need to see how our congregation's celebrations reflect that local diversity.

Epiphany. Traditionally, Epiphany points to the spread of the church from beyond the bounds of Israel to those who were of different cultures. The magi were not Jews, yet they recognized and worshiped the newborn Messiah. He was significant for them, not only for Israel. The New Testament bears witness to the tension involved in the decision to admit the Gentiles to full membership in the church without requiring them to become Jews first, but the necessity of that decision is pointed to from the very beginning, with the visit of the magi.

As the celebrations developed in the medieval West, the number of magi was fixed at three, and names were given, although scripture knew nothing of this specificity. More than that, however, tradition assigned different cultures to those three. Usually one appeared quite northern European, one Mongolian, and the third Ethiopian. Clearly the gospel was intended for "the ends of the earth." Most of us who are Christians in this country probably can identify with one of those traditional magi, since we come from the Gentile world and are included in the church because of its global mission in past generations.

The church has emphasized global mission in the days following Epiphany, and that fitted well with the theological character of the season. To be "a light to the nations" and therefore in mission to the world is a significant part of Epiphany. We need also to celebrate the results of past mission and the mature churches that have grown from such missions and now participate with us in global witness.

Lent and Easter (and Baptism). It is difficult to speak of the Easter season, with its preparation in Lent and Holy Week, without mentioning the relationship of baptism to the theme of global witness. Early Christians understood Lent as the time of final preparation of candidates for baptism and the recommitment of those already baptized. Baptisms normally occurred on Easter Eve, as the candidates joined in dying with Christ so that they might also be raised with him. Lenten and Easter ceremonies have wide cultural variations, even as Christmas ones do, precisely because of the cultures into which the church has entered. The same study and evaluation needs to be done of these customs as has been mentioned in the Christmas season. There is also the same usefulness of drawing on the customs of the church in other cultures in order to show the global character of the church.

Baptism at this season points to the fact that Christians are also called to follow the way of the cross. Our recognition of the redemption wrought by Jesus, the supreme example of the Suffering Servant, should lead to our own willingness to be such suffering servants in our own setting, if that should be the task to which we are called. In our own society at the moment, such a calling may not be common. The Lenten season can therefore be used to help a congregation understand and intercede for Christians in various situations around the world whose faith is being tested by suffering and persecution. Writings from such Christians, visits by Christians from those churches, or the establishment of links by way of sister congregations can be pursued. Many denominations have channels for developing these bonds and guidelines for making them fruitful. Were we to see how other Christians live out their faith in very difficult situations we might recognize ways in which we have avoided even mild forms of disapproval, shunning the way of the cross.

Baptism is the sign of the engrafting of the newly baptized into the risen Christ, becoming part of the one body. It is this body that is global in character. If there is an Easter Eve celebration of the renewal of baptismal vows, there could be a sharp focus on the global character of the one body to which we have been joined by this sacrament. Baptism also points to the priestly character of the covenant people, and that in turn shows the calling and the privilege of God's people to pray for others in intercessory prayer. These others can obviously be part of the household of faith, but they can also be those who do not know God and who therefore cannot pray for themselves. Part of the "priesthood of all believers" is lived out when we pray for the needs of the whole world, for the areas at war, for the hungry and the oppressed, for those who suffer all forms of injustice, wherever they may be. To the degree that we are specific in our prayers, the global witness of the church will come into view for the local congregation.

Easter is also the source of our mission. We are the people who know of the resurrection. It is the risen Christ to whom all power and authority has been given and who therefore commands that his disciples "go . . . and make disciples of all nations" (Matt. 28:18–19). This emphasis culminates in Ascension Day and Pentecost.

Pentecost. The coming of the Spirit, as witnessed to in the book of Acts, leads directly to the mission of the church across cultural and language boundaries without destroying those languages. The church has no native language, nor was one created at Pentecost. Rather, the Spirit made it possible for Christians to be understood in the many languages that are native to the peoples of the world. The ability to communicate across this major cultural barrier—language—is part of the Spirit's leading into mission, with no boundaries given except "the ends of the earth." We see here God's intention that the church's witness be global. The celebration of Pentecost calls the local congregation to the renewal of its own vision of the church beyond itself. It is the season to renew the commitment to come into contact with Christians around the world and to find means to do so. The increasing ethnic pluralism in our own local communities can assist us in this task.

For churches in our own country, Pentecost comes at the beginning of the summer season, a time when conferences, travel, and vacations are significant parts of congregational realities. In some congregations, it could be useful to help those who are traveling to make contact with churches in different countries, or to plan for attendance at conferences where there will be Christians from other parts of the world. For children, the summer programs of the local church could also be an opportunity to learn about children growing up in churches in other parts of the world. The possibilities are there, but it takes a church that has a global vision to make the best use of them—and to bring back what individuals have learned to share with the rest of the congregation. A structured time of reporting in the fall could help the whole congregation benefit from the variety of experiences that all age groups have had over the summer.

World Communion Sunday (the Eucharist). The first Sunday in October is designated World Communion Sunday. The celebration of the Eucharist always points to the gathering of Christians around a common Lord at a common table. The special celebration on this Sunday points quite directly to that global emphasis. It should not be neglected at other celebrations of the Lord's Supper throughout the year, however.

The Lord's Supper points not only to the global extension of the church as a reality in our time but also to the coming kingdom, the final reign of God. Therefore, the eschatological character of the Eucharist needs to be considered.

Christ the King. This Sunday immediately before Advent and the beginning of Advent are the major times of eschatological emphasis in the liturgical year. In the book of Revelation, as well as elsewhere in scripture, the goal of God's intention for history is pictured as a holy city. It will be inhabited by those from all tribes and nations. There is no hint of the eventual overcoming of cultural differences, but only of the elimination of conflict, hatred, and tension due to them. The city will have a cosmopolitan, global character about it. The Communion service points even now to that eschatological reality, and the table at which we gather is the foretaste of that heavenly banquet. The global character of that final feast points to the global character of our present celebrations. If people "will come from east and west, and from north and south, and sit at table in the kingdom of God" (Luke 13:29), then even now we need to remember the Christians who gather at tables around the world, as we gather in our own congregation. Special offerings taken at Communion services can also be directed on some occasions toward the global witness that this particular congregation is making to those Christians around the world who stand in particular need of our assistance.

Theological Resources

Several biblical and theological themes have been mentioned, and four need to be listed more specifically.

The nature of the church as catholic. This affirmation points beyond, or at least adds, a global perspective to the understanding of church unity or ecumenicity. A local congregation in our society can readily lose sight of these other churches and assume that they need play no part in the day-to-day life of the congregation. If the perspectives of these other Christians or examples from their lives can be included in the preaching, then the congregation is helped to understand what it means to be part of the larger church. If members of the congregation are urged to meet Christians from other parts of the world, that will reinforce and support what is attempted along this line in the preaching and the intercessory prayers.

It would be particularly helpful to be aware of churches in situations that are not comfortable, where difficult choices have to be made and persecution is possible. This could help Christians in the United States realize the full significance of a faith that can both lead to suffering and can triumph in the midst of such suffering. First Peter 5:8–9 speaks directly to the community of faith, which is worldwide and which may be called upon to suffer. Revelation 7:9–17 recalls the martyrs "from every nation, from all tribes and peoples and tongues." Such themes are particularly appropriate in the Lenten season.

The mission of the church as global. It is through a sympathy for world mission that many Christians in our country have been brought to a realization of the worldwide character of the church. Such mission needs to continue, but with the awareness of the work of the global church in this enterprise. The promise to Abraham included the blessing of all the nations through the descendants of Abraham and Sarah (Gen. 22:18). The task of the covenant people is expressed in the imagery of being "a light to the nations" (Isa. 42:6; 49:6; 55:4–5, related to Israel; Luke 2:30–32, applied to Jesus; Matt. 5:14–16, applied to the disciples).

It is very interesting to note the eschatological passages of Isaiah 2:1–4 and 25:6 and Revelation 21:23–26, which tell of the final fulfillment of the role of "light to the Gentiles." What is interesting is that "the nations" remain, even in the eschaton. There seems to be no thought that national identities will be wiped out. Yet clearly, by adhering to the "law of God," the nations will be at peace with one another. It would be interesting to ask congregation members if their view of heaven includes nations or peoples of various cultures or whether they somehow assume the life to come will eliminate all such differences. If the future life for which we devoutly hope includes such diversity, we would do well to learn to live with such realities in the church now. Such an awareness could also put under judgment modern forms of nationalism that cannot take into account the covenant community that is drawn from all nations and yet preserves national identities.

The incarnation. That God the creator could come to be a part of this creation, entering into our human life as one of us, is an astonishing statement. Yet this is what we celebrate at Christmas. To take on human flesh meant also to take on human culture—to speak a particular language, to live in a particular society with its history and its customs. Granted the choice of which culture had to do with the covenant people and its hard-learned understanding of the ways of God, yet the incarnation shows the possibility of combining God's real presence in the midst of history and the preservation of the integrity of human culture. Nor was that presence without a radical judgment on the ways in which that culture had vitiated or twisted the will of God already revealed.

Some biblical passages related to these incarnational themes are Matthew 1:1–17 and 2:1–2 and Luke 2:1–7 and 3:23–38, which give the specific human genealogy of Jesus and the historical context of his birth. In John 6:41–42 the issue is raised differently: How can one whose parents and lineage are known to the community be also from God?

The issue of the admission of Gentiles into the church was a major turning point for the young church. The task of relating to a wide variety of human cultures—preserving and judging each of them—continued this incarnational paradigm. Always the temptation is either to ignore the culture and attempt some nonincarnate form of the faith or to refuse to judge and therefore accommodate to the culture in ways that deny the faith. The church always needs to struggle to maintain its proper balance.

The task is made both more necessary and more possible if we are in touch with the church in other cultures. Christians from outside of our culture can raise questions for us—helping us to avoid the dangers mentioned. They can mention possibilities of authentic "taking on" of elements in our culture that we have not seen, and they can point out the need for judgment on areas that we have too readily adopted. Mutual respect and bonds across national and cultural lines can help us all to be more faithful.

Various passages on the unity of the body of Christ across such lines are important, such as Galatians 3:27–28, Colossians 3:11, and 2 Corinthians 8:1–15. The difficult struggle to determine what is necessary to the gospel and what can be altered in a new cultural situation can be seen in Acts 15:1–35 and Galatians 2:1–14.

Creation. Foundational to all the doctrines that have been mentioned thus far is the basic understanding of God as the creator of all that is. Because God has created the world God seeks the redemption of the world, choosing a people to help in this process. Above all, Jesus is Lord of all, not because he has captured the world away from an alien creator but because he is also the God who has created this world. He has been Lord from the beginning. By his cross and resurrection he has freed the world from its bondage to alien powers that had not created it. It is the Creator who redeems. God is concerned for the whole world, not just the church. We pray for the whole world because we are called to love it as God loves it. The church makes a global witness because the God whom it serves is a global God, by both creation and redemption. Colossians 1:13–20 shows this connection. The creeds insist that the God who created heaven and earth is the same God who became incarnate for its redemption.

An Example Text

Many passages that relate to particular aspects of this topic have already been mentioned. However, let us now deal with a passage not mentioned before, one that is not directly associated with a particular time in the liturgical year or with one of the sacraments: Psalm 96.

In the lectionary, Psalm 96 is suggested for Christmas Day, probably because of verses 12b–13a:

> Then shall all the trees of the wood
>   sing for joy
> before the LORD, for he comes,
> for he comes to judge the earth.

The whole text is thirteen verses. In that fairly brief space, in the Revised Standard Version, the terms "the nations" and "the peoples" are used seven times, and the phrases "all the earth," "the earth," and "the world" are used five times. The perspective is clearly global. God is the creator of all of this, of the peoples of all nations, not only Israel, and of the earth with its trees and oceans. This God is not only the creator of all but also the One who judges with righteousness and truth.

The psalm points to the concern of God for the whole world and for justice among all the nations. The incarnation is the new way that God has instituted for the carrying out of this concern. The psalm would point the church to God's concern for all peoples and for justice throughout the earth. Verses 10 and 13b could be useful as part of a call to prayer for the world or in the prayers themselves. Verses 12b–13a, used at Christmas, point to the intention of the incarnation as furthering this concern for a just world. In churches where Christmas is seen in more individualistic and spiritual terms, this would be a helpful corrective.

The basic theme of the psalm is praise, and all the peoples of the earth are called on to praise the one true God, the creator of all. The fact that not all people do praise God leads directly to the need for our witness worldwide. Furthermore, when we praise God, we are doing so in one sense on behalf of the whole world, as those priestly representatives of God's creation who can praise. Our mission is to help all the rest of the world enter into praise with us.

This psalm could be used as the text for a sermon in an unusual way. It could be printed in the bulletin as a unison reading—or used from the responsive readings in a hymnal—breaking the reading into two sections, verses 1–9 and 10–13. The sermon would then follow each reading, letting the people see the text. Verses 1–9 stress the universal work of God in creation and salvation, which are of concern to all the world, not only to the covenant people. All are called to worship this God. The intention of world mission to create worshiping congregations around the world would be helpful in showing the corporate and global nature of the church.

The second section, verses 10–13, indicates that God is concerned for equity, for righteousness, and for truth. The global worship that is the goal of mission is a worship that leads to righteous actions, to truth in our dealings with one another around the world. Even though the nations are not yet able to live in this fashion, the global church is called on to be a witness to what this would mean. We in the church are called to live with equity, with righteousness, and with truth across the national lines that divide our world into armed camps and antagonistic alliances. How do we live as global witnesses to God's intention for the whole world? Could this be a costly witness for many Christians? For us?

After the sermon, the prayers of the people could then lift up specific areas of the world to be prayed for, as well as different parts of the church.

Psalm 96 could be geared more specifically to certain seasons of the year, including Advent and Epiphany. It could be used in a baptismal service, to show the nature of the body to which the baptized are engrafted. It would probably best be used at a time other than Christmas, since that day should stress the marvel of the incarnation itself. My own choice would probably be Advent, since the psalm picks up themes proper to that time, but it could then be used as a psalm at Christmas without preaching on it, in the hope that the sermon in Advent would have planted these wider themes in the mind of the congregation.

5

Preaching About Work— Deepest Labor and Deepest Rest

Don M. Wardlaw

In 1882 Peter McGuire, founder of the United Brotherhood of Carpenters, suggested a holiday to honor the working people of the United States. McGuire led what amounted to the first Labor Day parade down the streets of New York City in September of that same year. In 1894 President Grover Cleveland signed a bill making the first Monday in September Labor Day, a legal holiday. Puerto Rico and Canada have joined the United States in the same holiday, with Australia calling its special day Eight Hour Day, commemorating the successful struggle for a shorter working day. But today Labor Day weekend has become for most of these populations more of an excuse for rest and recreation than an occasion to celebrate the human right to decent wages and working conditions. Labor Day weekend has become, in North America, three days for the final fling of summer, a time for the last water-ski and the closing of the summer cottage. Few people on a Labor Day weekend picnic would prefer a speech by a labor chief to feeding the ducks or playing softball.

A Labor Day Word

Whatever the popular perception of Labor Day, the preacher who tunes in on the theological import of Labor Day will find enough profound pulpit values to feed the faithful on Labor Day Sunday as well as on a month of Sundays thereafter.

The Labor Day word can be about work as an ordinance of creation, or work as a blessing rather than a curse, or work as a human response to God's call. The word for workers can celebrate the human right to decent wages, hours, and working conditions. Sermons that help parishioners fathom the meaning of their toil can focus on industrial and economic life as calling, or on government, law, and politics as vocation, or on marriage and homemaking as sacred work.

Whatever the angle on the sanctity of labor, each approach fundamentally seeks to answer the basic human cry for release from the burden of repetitive, grinding toil. Ordinarily the word "labor" conjures archetypal visions of sweat, muscle, and blood, hammer and anvil, sledge on rock, coolies carving out a railroad, a plowboy straining behind his mules. In the words of the writer of Genesis, "In the sweat of your face you shall eat bread" (Gen. 3:19a). The deeper echoes of Labor Day carry primordial cries for freedom from soul-dulling, incessant travail. We hear that plea in the sighs of children in the early factories, of miners who rarely see the light of day, of assembly-line workers narcose from their robotlike moves.

Labor for Self-Esteem

Talk of ceaseless slogging, however, would remain relatively limited were we to relegate it to the industrial grind alone. While many of our parishioners still feel imprisoned by repetitive toil at computer terminals, switchboards, and filing cabinets, the great majority of us—preachers included—are trapped in a grinding labor of the spirit that dehumanizes as surely as if we were sledging stones fourteen hours a day in a deep quarry. Such toil is the struggle for self-esteem, the deepest, most painful labor in the human experience. We need to explore the kind of preaching that can offer the deepest rest as release from the deepest labor.

Jesus had this fundamental, desperate striving for self-esteem in mind one day when he looked down on the crowd that had come out from Chorazin, Bethsaida, and Capernaum to hear him. These were ordinary people who were struggling under the Jewish law to feel good about themselves. These were folk burdened by the sense that their best was never good enough for God, people weighted by the wearisome list of their wrongs that priests held before them, souls borne down by the need to scheme to impress Yahweh with their goodness.

As Jesus stood before these upturned faces, he must have spied a familiar scene on the far side of the field down below. Two yoked oxen were struggling ahead of a plow. Jesus' practiced eye told him instantly that the oxen were heavy laden because of a poorly fitting yoke. The patient beasts' halting, twitching movements betrayed nagging pain from the raw flesh beneath the rubbing yoke. Jesus looked down again at the people. They had come to him because the yoke the established church had given them was no better fitting or useful than the wooden frame that galled the oxen's necks. This yoke that chafed the people consisted of six hundred commandments and prohibitions about everything from the cleanser to be used on eating utensils to the proper rope for drawing a bucket from the well. The people had been raised to believe that the yoke of these statutes would lighten their load of guilt and despair about their worth before God. Yet for all their concern about proper prayer posture, habits of dress and speech, rituals of cleanliness and appearances of godliness, they were doomed from the start with the wrong yoke. This yoke only added to rather than lessened the burden. In compassion for them in their halting, twitching labors for wholeness beneath the Law, Jesus offered them the promise of deepest rest:

> Come to me, all who *labor* and are heavy laden, and I will give you rest. Take my yoke upon you, and learn from me; for I am gentle and lowly in heart, and you will find rest for your souls. For my yoke is easy, and my burden is light.
>
> Matthew 11:28–30, emphasis added

The Labor of the Co-Dependent

Jesus' promise today of release from the grinding labor for self-esteem could well read, "Come to me, all you *co-dependents,* and I will give you rest." For the essence of the co-dependent's struggle is an unending toil for a clear sense of identity and self-esteem.

Co-dependence is a relatively new term in the field of chemical dependency, used originally to define the condition of
the spouse of an alcoholic. Ann Wilson Schaef, Sharon
Wegscheider-Cruse, and others who work in chemical dependency, mental health, family therapy, and the women's
movement have now expanded the conceptualization of co-
dependence to refer to it as a subsyndrome of a broad social
illness called the addictive process.[1] We can be addicted, not
just to alcohol, drugs, food, and nicotine, but also to everything from dieting to gossip, from power lust to "cling-clung"
relationships, from personal cleanliness to obsession with
money—even to religion. Any time we feel compelled to deny
such dependence, we are in fact caught in an addictive process.
Schaef sums it up succinctly: "An addiction, in short, is any
substance or process we feel we have to lie about."[2]

However ominous our battles with our addictions, a yet
more insidious struggle waits for us pastors and our people in
co-dependence. We are co-dependent when we cooperate, unwittingly or otherwise, with someone near to us who is caught
in an addictive process. We co-dependents are most visible as
heroic yet troubled caretakers. We are addicted to rescuing the
addicted. A joke making the rounds among recovery people
asks, "What flashes before the eyes of the co-dependent who
is about to die?" The answer: "Someone else's life!" We co-
dependents apologize for the addict's problem, lie in order to
cover it up, blame the addict's struggle on ourselves ("If only
I'd change, they'd change"), strive mightily in all circumstances to save the addict. We co-dependents make good
"messiahs."[3] We aim to please, often with embarrassing cost
to ourselves and others. In neglecting our own loved ones to
ride off at the drop of a hat to help another, or in turning every
social situation into an excuse to get wrapped up in another's
feelings, we often exacerbate more than ease the other person's addiction.

Three characteristics belong to all this co-dependent labor
to save others. First, we are prone to control and impress,
whether we are protectors manipulating information or rescu-
ers reinforcing feelings of helplessness in the addicted. Second, we generally keep a distance from those we seek to help.
As counselor we seem to be more comfortable in the role of

the answer-person; as crusader, one who reserves passion for issues more than for people; as teacher, an information giver. Third, we tend to deny our real feelings by working mainly within a framework of rationality, what Alcoholics Anonymous bluntly calls "stinkin' thinkin.' " We offer ready reasons for the false face we use to try to make others happy or the circumlocutions we use to avoid talking straight with the patient about cancer. If your experience is as mine, you recognize yourself in some or many of these characteristics. Estimates on the extent of co-dependence in the United States range up to 96 percent of the population, with the percentage running higher among the helping professions.[4]

The Root of the Problem

Jesus' offer to help us out from under this chafing yoke has a ring of deep compassion. He is appealing to a cowering child deep within us, one who hungers for nurture and identity. As Carmen Berry says, co-dependents "tend to give to others what they desperately need to receive themselves."[5] The profile on any co-dependent starts with an emotionally repressive family. As children we co-dependents were not often allowed to identify our legitimate needs, let alone address them. We may have grown up in a large family or been raised by a single parent. We may have known our parents more by their absence than presence, whether they both worked or were chronically ill physically or emotionally or shunted us off to residential schools. In every case our needs were lost to their needs.

In defense against this galling yoke of parental neglect, the little child within us developed a secret self-centered agenda known clinically as a narcissistic personality disorder. In the early years we began entertaining unrealistic images of our abilities, power, intelligence, and appearance in order to win more attention from our parents. But this exalted view rarely worked. Our craving for praise today still won't go away. Relatively minor failures still threaten the delicate tissue of our identity.

But the deepest wound at the heart of our narcissism is a loss of a clear sense of the boundaries between self and others.

Writes psychotherapist Thomas Maeder, "Narcissists were deprived in infancy and childhood of the affection and the deep emotional interactions with their parents that would have allowed the normal development of a distinct sense of the difference between self and other and a feeling of personal value."[6] Hence, all these years when we have responded rather impulsively to the distress signals of others, we have to a great extent been unconsciously answering the alarm bell of our own pain. That's why we have trouble at times genuinely giving or receiving love. We have been too absorbed in cleaning up others' messes to stop long enough to feel our own chaos. We must keep on rescuing, pleasing, and giving in order to keep from feeling worthless and abandoned.

Preaching to Co-Dependents

Preaching *as* co-dependents *to* co-dependents is a formidable challenge when we understand that the church, along with the school and family, is one of our basic institutions that is built upon and exacerbates some of the key attributes of co-dependence. Co-dependents are in the majority in most congregations and clerical gatherings. The "niceness" and moral perfectionism valued by the average congregation pushes us all to be heroic caretakers whether we are equipped for that role or not. When we preachers step into the pulpit we hope to offer not only a word of grace for co-dependents but also a word of apology for how the church has "bound heavy burdens, hard to bear, and laid them on people's shoulders" (Matt. 23:4, alt.). The word we need to hear and want to share as co-dependents is the same as Jesus' word for those who struggled under the yoke of the Law: "Come to me, all who *labor* and are heavy laden, and I will give you rest."

Preaching Under a Chafing Yoke

But what we want to offer from the pulpit and what we in fact submit are often two different things. Frequently when we remain unaware of our own co-dependent's yoke, we are prone to preach sermons that unwittingly promote co-dependence in our hearers. We prescribe right conduct ("We've got to love

the unlovely!"), or right ideals ("Oh, where is good, old-fash-
ioned honesty today?"), or right beliefs ("Unless you cling to
Christ, you are nowhere!"), with little or no reference to the
faith resources that enable human transformation to take
place. These are hortatory sermons (meaning, to incite), ma-
joring in imperatives while ignoring the indicatives (God's part
in the matter) that empower the reconstituted life. However
good our intentions with such preaching, we nevertheless do
violence to people's souls. These sermons are marked with
characteristics of our own co-dependence. We are trying to
control our people's lives by prescribing their attitudes and
behavior. We inadvertently put our congregation at a distance
by demanding of them what they cannot deliver. We have all
the right reasons ("stinkin' thinkin' ") for asking of our people
what we in reality are afraid to admit we cannot produce.

This kind of preaching is the last thing co-dependents need
to hear. It only puts more weight on an already poorly fitting
yoke. It provokes the hearers to newer strivings to please while
ignoring their muffled cries for love and acceptance. It pushes
the people to manipulate their world to look good before God
and fellow church members. So often when we preachers get
caught up in these hortatory impulses, we become unavailable,
ironically, to the word of grace in the sermon's scriptural passage that could help unlock all us co-dependents from our
deepest pain. The psalmist knew the futility of any such attempts to live the gracious life without the anchoring Presence
that enables it:

> Unless the LORD builds the house,
>   those who build it *labor in vain.* . . .
> In vain . . you rise up early and go late to rest,
>   eating the bread of anxious toil.
> > > Psalm 127:1a–2, emphasis added

The Preacher's Own Chafing Yoke

When we preachers press our people into further co-
dependent behavior, we most often are projecting our own
unclaimed co-dependence onto the pew. Therapists who

counsel clergy have begun to notice a significant problem common to a large number of ministers. Many of us pastors were raised firstborn, or as an only child, or were treated like an only child. We were rushed through childhood as little adults without the warm, encircling love we needed and deserved. Consequently, we grew up feeling that others' delight in us depended on our hard work and responsibility. Thomas Maeder, who works with disturbed "people helpers," pictures such struggling clergy.

> They have a chronically low sense of self-worth and a stunted ability to receive genuine love or friendship from others; only their *selfishly selfless labors* make them feel satisfied with themselves. As a result, they may be driven into a veritable frenzy of wholesale helping, which is motivated not by altruism but by a desperate need to fill an inner vacancy.[7]

An Episcopal priest who as a Jungian analyst treats many clergy describes the problem.

> They give too much without knowing how to take. . . . They build up even more of an inhibition against being able to appropriately take things for themselves. . . . They are into loving their God and loving their neighbor, but they forget that little, crucial, additional thing: "as thyself."[8]

If during the week we clergy find ourselves opening the study door every time there's a knock or running with help every time we hear a heavy sigh, chances are we shall on Sundays in our sermons demand, however subtly, that same kind of driven behavior from our parishioners. If in our pastoral toil we, like a paschal lamb, take into our bodies and souls the chaos of the congregation, often acquiring as a result ulcers, colitis, high blood pressure, and even cancer, we more than likely will call in our sermons for our people to take on unquestioningly the tumult that surrounds them. Here we are loading onto our people's shoulders the same kind of ill-fitting yoke that we wear. And to the practiced eye and ear we are exposing in our anxious labor in the pulpit our deeper needs as co-dependents. We are using the pulpit to *seek* rather than to express wholeness.

Preaching Under a Comfortable Yoke

But grace abounds for us sinners in the pulpit! Another kind of yoke is available for us to help us bear the weight of our co-dependence. This yoke enables us to start dealing with our own co-dependence and thus to come to a much better position to help our people deal with theirs.

Legend has it that if a Galilean farmer of the early first century wanted the best yoke for his oxen, he would have it cut and shaped by a certain carpenter of Nazareth named Jesus. From the far reaches of the province farmers came to this master craftsman for the shaping and smoothing of yokes that made load-bearing easy. Christ still offers us the yoke that fits. "Take my yoke upon you, and learn from me; for I am gentle and lowly in heart, and you will find rest for your souls. For my yoke is easy, and my burden is light."

Deepest rest for our preacher's deepest labor in co-dependence begins when we take onto our shoulders Christ's yoke. Once under this dual yoke as Christ's partner ("take *my* yoke upon *you*"), we enter into a Christ-dependence that sparks a personal transformation that begins to defuse and demobilize our co-dependence. To be yoked to Christ is to be soul companion with the authentic self God intends for us to be. In that confederacy we begin losing our co-dependent need to strive to fill an inner vacancy through attention-getting caretaking.

This yoked Presence can offer itself in genuine human loves and friendships that honor our deepest needs and ask us to be only who we are. Maybe it comes through a spouse who insists that the marriage be a partnership rather than a rescue mission, a union that starts making obsolete all our fantastic monuments to ourselves. Maybe this Presence encounters us in the trust and truthfulness of a therapist who helps us begin making peace with parents who used us more than delighted in us. Perhaps we know the Presence in a recovery or support group that lovingly confronts us while offering us the mother's or father's gleam that we never knew.

Maybe the Christ-partner comes to us intrapsychically, emerging from our unconscious through our dream life, offering us through dream images a vision of our centered self that does not need to awe others to justify our existence. Possibly the dream figure is what Carl Jung would call our inner shadow, our tribal brother or loving sister who when yoked to our ego gives us a hopeful glimpse of our fullness as a person.[9] Maybe in prayer and meditation we begin opening to a Presence through images given to the inner eye of new visions of harmony in the face of the old potential for pomposity.

Under the Christ-yoke we begin walking to a new beat with a new kind of intentionality. Our co-dependence begins to lose its edge. The old drive to manage information and manipulate others' need diminishes. We are increasingly more comfortable down on the same level as others, less afraid of the mutuality and intimacy with them that enable us to enjoy our authentic gifts and to confront our genuine weaknesses. We depend less and less on a brittle rationality and more and more on a feeling life that no longer cowers in the shadows with our wounded child.

From this changing life come transformed sermons. Our sermons now offer the possibility of a yoked Presence rather than the burden of oppressive demands. As we get more free from the shackles of our own co-dependence, we are also becoming liberated from the need to play upon the "duty strings" of our people's co-dependence. We do not tell our hearers that they have got to do anything. Instead, we *de*scribe rather than *pre*scribe. We picture ways this gracious yoked Presence offers them the acceptance and nurture that has been missing in their lives. We try to show them how grace relieves them of any necessity to sparkle with niceness and good works in order to win self-esteem. We declare that in the Christ-yoke they are esteemed already, that their grinding labor of rescuing, pleasing, and protecting others to gain self-worth is no longer viable or necessary. Ironically, when we preach this freedom from the co-dependent desperation our hearers will be more prone to want "to do something," not because we pressure them to do it, but because the grace they experience through the images and visions we offer draws them into joyous action. Now they wear a yoke that fits. Exclaims Bernard of Clairvaux of Jesus' yoke, "O blessed burden that makes all burdens light, O blessed yoke that bears the bearer up!" Or, as Augustine claimed of Christ's yoke, "This burden is not the weight upon one that is laden, but the wing of one that is about to fly."

Notes

1. Ann Wilson Schaef, *Co-Dependence: Misunderstood-Mistreated* (San Francisco: Harper & Row, 1986); Ann Wilson Schaef, *When Society Becomes an Addict* (San Francisco: Harper & Row, 1987); Ann Wilson Schaef and Diane Fassel, *The Addictive Organization* (San Francisco: Harper & Row, 1988); Sharon Wegscheider-Cruse, ed., *Co-Dependency* (Deerfield Beach, Fla.: Health Communications, 1988); Carmen Renee Berry, *When Helping You Is Hurting Me: Escaping the Messiah Trap* (San Francisco: Harper & Row, 1988).

2. Schaef, *Co-Dependence*, p. 24.

3. Carmen Renee Berry, in her book, *When Helping You Is Hurting Me: Escaping the Messiah Trap*, lists seven types of messiahs who function as co-dependents: pleaser, rescuer, giver, counselor, protector, teacher, and crusader.

4. Schaef and Fassel, *The Addictive Organization*, p. 96.

5. Berry, *When Helping You Is Hurting Me*, p. 57.

6. Thomas Maeder, "Wounded Healers," *Atlantic Monthly*, January 1989, p. 45.

7. Ibid., p. 41 (emphasis added).

8. Quoted by Maeder, "Wounded Healers," p. 41.

9. For more on this, see Robert A. Johnson, *Innerwork* (San Francisco: Harper & Row, 1986), pp. 42–50.

6

Preaching About Evangelism— Faith Finding Its Voice

Thomas G. Long

Some years ago I agreed, at the urging of a congregational Christian education committee, to teach a church school discussion class on the topic of evangelism. This was in a church with a long history of strong, prophetic, and sacrificial urban ministry. It saw itself—and rightly so, I think—as a church committed to the sort of issues and people that many softer, safer congregations often ignore. On the first day of the course, I arrived at my classroom early and was taping a sign that read EVANGELISM CLASS on the door. A member of the congregation who happened to be passing down the hallway noticed the sign, wrinkled his nose in slight disdain, and said, "What in the world are you going to say about *that?*"

I knew what he meant. In fact, I had spent a good deal of time myself wondering just what I was going to say about *that.* "Evangelism" is for many people, frankly, a nose-wrinkling word, a term they hold in approximately the same regard as the phrase "professional wrestling." Both are considered to be activities that draw large, uncritical crowds, involve a measure of sham, work on irrational emotions, and could end up hurting somebody.

Maybe part of the problem has to do with the word itself: evangelism. "Ism" words can sometimes refer to practices, such as criticism, plagiarism, or, more positively, baptism. Much of the time, though, ism words refer to social movements and have about them the aroma of ideological strife and party politics, as in sectarianism, liberalism, elitism, or communism. Moreover, "isms" imply "ists," cells of true believers who devotedly practice the ism, such as anarchists, Maoists, terrorists, or fundamentalists. Small wonder, then, that many church people come to think of evangelism as a kind of partisan activity practiced only by a cadre of special zealots called evangelists.

The problem about evangelism is deeper than language, though. We must admit that some Christians have said and done things in the name of evangelism that betray the very gospel they seek to share. I do not refer merely to the fact that "TV evangelist" has become a label of ridicule, a punch line on late-night talk shows. Virtually every thinking person recognizes the difference between the electronic circus tents erected by preachers of greed and the work of the historic Christian church. I am referring more to the fact that well-meaning Christians who are convinced they have a gospel worth sharing with others have often been tempted to forget that the people with whom they share it are also of worth to God. The result is that the good news gets communicated by bad news methods—pushy, obnoxious, and insensitive.

"The task of the Christian witness," states theologian John Leith, "is on the one hand to proclaim the message with integrity and, on the other hand, to help those who believe to understand how Jesus Christ answers the deepest questions of their lives and illuminates and makes sense of their experience."[1] This means that evangelical witness occurs in an environment of respect, both for the gospel and for the questions and experiences of those to whom it is told. D. T. Niles's famous definition of evangelism, "One beggar telling another beggar where to find food,"[2] is both poetic and apt so long as the church sees itself in a position of weakness: that is, as a beggar. But when the church attempts to flex cultural and social muscle in the name of evangelism, its efforts can become coercive and oppressive. Some Christians, who would never dream of kicking down their neighbors' doors and barging uninvited into their homes, nevertheless somehow see the Great Commission as a license to intrude without welcome into others' lives and to trample thoughtlessly upon their concerns and convictions.

Evangelism, then, may be a questionable term, and it has surely gotten a bad name in some quarters. So what in the world are we going to say about *that?*

Laryngitis in the House of Faith

We must begin by trying to reclaim the word "evangelism." In the largest sense, evangelism means living the gospel in ways that can be seen, heard, and felt, and, as such, it embraces every aspect of the church's life. Whenever a community of faith embodies the good news of Jesus Christ in its education, service, and ministries of compassion and social confrontation, it is engaging in forms of evangelism.

It is important, however, to think of evangelism not only in this larger sense but also in the more particular sense of communicating the faith in words to those who are outside the faith. Even this more restricted form of evangelism is not a sectarian ideology, nor is it the partisan practice of a few glassy-eyed evangelical activists. Properly understood, it is a normal outgrowth of the life of faith and an activity of the whole church. Put simply, evangelism involves people who believe the gospel, God's story, telling it to others in ways that they can hear and understand it. Sometimes this story is told to people who have never heard it before, and sometimes it is told to people who *have* heard it, but who do not trust it because they have not *truly* heard it, not heard it in ways they can understand, or because they find it unbelievable, irrelevant, boring, or even confining and oppressive.

The stakes are high, since the Christian church knows of no other way to transmit the faith from generation to generation than by someone's having the conviction and the courage to try to put it into the kind of words that others can hear and understand. Whenever anyone begins to believe the gospel and to make it the center of his or her life, it is because someone else was willing to try to stammer out in words what the faith means. The theological concept of the word of God has been the subject of much sophisticated theological discussion, but no theology of the word can distance itself from the basic truth that the gospel is communicated in human words—frail and halting human speech.

Having said this, we must be careful not to paint too simple a picture of the way people come to hear and to trust the gospel. Sometimes we imagine that evangelism takes place in only one fairly linear process: church people go to unchurched people and tell them the gospel; some of them believe it and thus become involved themselves in the church. That can happen, of course, but much of the time people become enmeshed in the life of the church before they have anything like a working knowledge of the gospel. Theologian George Lindbeck has observed that early converts to Christianity "did not, for the most part, first understand the faith and then decide to become Christians; rather, the process was reversed: they first decided and then they understood. More precisely, they were first attracted by the Christian community and form of life."[3]

What Lindbeck says of the early church remains true today. People are not attracted to an abstract message, disembodied from a community of people who believe, celebrate, and practice its claims. Even if they were, the gospel is not such a message. "The proclamation of the Christian gospel," Lindbeck says, " . . . may be first of all the telling of a story, but this gains power and meaning insofar as it is embodied in the total gestalt of community life and action."[4] In other words, evangelism in the narrower sense of sharing the gospel with those who do not believe is always connected to evangelism in the larger sense: namely, the totality of the church's corporate life.

Often people find themselves involved in the life of a Christian congregation, even if it is only as a soloist in the choir, as a worker in the night shelter, as a shortstop on the church softball team, or as a child brought by parents, long before they become curious or knowledgeable about the fabric of belief that holds that congregation together. People find themselves engaged in the work and worship of Christian churches for all sorts of reasons. The fact remains, though, that at some point along the way someone must speak the gospel to them— parent to child, friend to friend, neighbor to neighbor, preacher to hearer, teacher to student.

The crisis in evangelism is not, then, a crisis in method. The church is constantly attacking the problem of evangelism by inventing some new program or technique. These have their place, but they are merely the outgrowth of something more basic. The enduring problem with evangelism is a crisis of voice, the fact that the household of faith has developed kerygmatic laryngitis and lost its ability to bring its faith to oral expression.

Suppose that a few inmates in a prisoner-of-war camp have managed secretly to build a crude radio receiver out of a razor blade and scraps of wire. Gathered covertly around this radio late one night, they hear, through the static, a news report that an army of liberation is advancing steadily toward the camp and that their freedom is near. Now this small group has heard news of immense importance for the whole camp, and there is simply no question that it must be told to the other prisoners. The very nature of the news demands its telling; no one would dare suggest that this word of coming liberation be cherished privately and silently in their hearts. They all know it will be difficult and dangerous to tell this news because the powers that still rule the camp will resist and punish those they catch in the act of telling. Also, some of the prisoners will undoubtedly have become so hopelessly adjusted to their captivity, they will not believe this news when it is told to them. Still, the news must be told, and they will find the means to do it. Perhaps they will whisper it from prisoner to prisoner in the stillness of the night, or perhaps they will tap it out in code at the meal table, but they will tell it regardless.

The church needs to recover the keen awareness that the gospel is *news* and that the life of the church is called into being by that news and the urgency of its becoming known. It is always difficult and often dangerous to tell this news, because the powers that reign resist its telling. Still the news must be told. Moreover, it is easy to mistake the effects of the gospel—the fellowship of the church, the good works of the church—for the gospel itself. If we lose the sense of the gospel as news, we will inevitably lose our voice as well.

Evangelism and the Pulpit: The Court of the Gentiles

"The gospel is the good news about who God is and to whom therefore we belong," wrote Carl Michaelson. "Part of the gospel," he went on to say, "is the good news that God has

appointed a people called the church for the purpose of enjoy-
ing the [gospel] story and telling it to others."[5] Evangelism,
therefore, is the sum and substance of the life of the church
and cannot be restricted to any special time or season.

There are periods, however, when the explicit task of put-
ting the gospel into words that others can hear and understand
comes firmly into view. Advent, Epiphany, Easter, and Pentecost are times in the liturgical year that embody a particular
stress on evangelism. Also, seasons of denominational emphasis on Christian education, theological education, and mission
include evangelism as a major motif.

Evangelism enters the pulpit in two main ways: through
sermons that are themselves "evangelistic" and through sermons that aim at building up the ongoing lay ministry of evangelism by equipping the hearers to carry on the task of
evangelism. In regard to the first of these, it may seem strange
to think of preaching an evangelistic sermon in an "ordinary"
Sunday service. After all, Christian worship assumes the presence of a believing, confessing, serving community of faith. In
short, worship happens because the people in the pews on
Sunday have already, in some way, been "evangelized."

The truth of the matter, however, is that any Sunday congregation is an amazingly complex mixture of faith and doubt,
confidence and uncertainty, wisdom and sheer ignorance. "It
is instructive, if somewhat dismaying," states William Muehl,
"to realize how many of the men and women in the pews
almost did not come to church that morning. And that in all
probability most of them feel that they are there under false
pretenses, that everyone around them feels more confidently
Christian, less restlessly rebellious than they do themselves."[6]

In other words, we cannot draw a circle labeled "community
of faith" around the Sunday congregation and mark everything outside that circle "the world." There is a band of gray,
a contemporary "court of the Gentiles" full of seekers, questioners, and doubters in every service of worship, and from
week to week people in the Sunday flock move in and out of
that band of ambiguity.

How should a preacher respond to this? Imagine a family,
two parents and three children, who decide to adopt another

child, say a ten-year-old boy. Suddenly there is another face at the dinner table, a person who has his own life story and who knows nothing of the history of this new family of which he is now a part. He does not catch the inside family jokes, has no idea who Aunt Bessie is, and does not remember last summer's family vacation in Florida. Now on the one hand, it would be foolish to think that this family must stop telling those jokes, cease talking about Aunt Bessie, and burn the pictures of Fort Lauderdale. Drawing upon common memory is much of what it means to be a family, and there would be no recognizable family life without it. On the other hand, it would be unthinkably cruel to keep on doing these things in the same old ways, as if there were no new person present to take into account. So what the family will do is to engage in the same familiar activities, but in ways that open them to this new person present among them, this new son and brother. Some things will need to be explained; familiar stories will be carefully retold. The family will not abandon its language, blot out its memories, or stifle its cherished patterns. It will simply engage in all of them in the awareness of the presence of this one who is learning the family ways.

So it is with evangelistic preaching. The homiletical task is not to present to nonbelievers some schematic condensation of the plan of salvation, whatever that might be, or some set of spiritual laws abstracted from the life of the worshiping and serving Christian community. It is rather to make the stories, the memories, the vocabulary, and the ritual patterns of the household of God coherent and available to those who are unfamiliar with them. It is the kind of preaching which is addressed primarily to those who already trust the gospel but which, at the same time, says to those who overhear it, "This is for you, too. The household of God is not complete until you know that you also are a son . . . a daughter. You belong here."

This kind of preaching requires careful attention to what may be termed the teaching dimensions of sermons, but it also requires patience on the part of the preacher and the church. It is a hard lesson, but the church must learn to allow those who overhear the gospel to ignore or to reject it. The church must learn to be steadfast about speaking its truth in ways that invite the stranger to participate in it, even when most strangers find the church's message hopelessly irrelevant or mistake it for the most boring kind of conventional wisdom.

In his collection of essays on language *The Message in the Bottle,* novelist Walker Percy imagines two scientists, physicists at Los Alamos in the 1940s, who leave their laboratory one Sunday morning, having worked all night. They pass a church on their way home, and as they go by, they hear through the open door a few words of the gospel being preached: "Come, follow me." Now, Percy wonders, how will these scientists respond to these words of gospel summons? "Given the exhilarating climate of the transcending objectivity and comradeship which must have existed at the high tide of physics," he says, "it is hard to imagine a proposition which would have sounded more irrelevant than the standard sermon."[7]

Percy now imagines a third Los Alamos scientist, living fifty years later, long after the robust optimism of the earlier days has vanished. This scientist knows that he does not hold the Promethean fire in his hand; indeed, this man's world is poised between nuclear destruction and the numbing irrelevance of consumerism. He spends his time doing routine radiation counts on synthetic cow's milk. He is, in short, the man of despair so aptly described by Kierkegaard.

This scientist, too, passes by the same church, now in ruins. A priest rushes from the ruins and engages the man in a modern paraphrase of Jesus' word to the woman at the well, climaxing in the same call to "Come, follow me." "It is possible," says Percy, "that a different kind of communication event occurs in the door of the church than occurred fifty years earlier." The beckoning of the gospel—"Come!"—is, claims Percy, a summons that is only relevant to a person in a certain predicament.[8]

The gospel must be preached in ways that can be understood by those who do not yet trust it, but it must be done in full recognition that when people do not sense their deep predicament, the gospel will often be heard as irrelevant. But the church is patient, waiting for the inevitable time when message and predicament will intersect. Now, admittedly, this is a nondramatic portrait of evangelistic preaching. Only rarely will it result in persons making sharp breaks with the past, sawdust-trail-style conversions. Rather, it patiently invites people to come confidently to the dinner table, to occupy the empty chairs at the banquet of God, to come to the places that have been held waiting for them, to learn to relish the rhythms of the stories lovingly told there, and to hear the word "God" as a word of deep cheer.

Evangelism and the Pulpit: Finding a Faithful Voice

The second way in which evangelism enters the pulpit is through sermons that build up the capacity of Christian people to speak the good news in their everyday lives. The task of the preacher is not only to preach in ways that can be heard and understood by those who are seekers and questioners, but also to equip those who are part of the active Christian community to find their voices in the world and to bear witness to the gospel in their everyday communication with others. This does not mean that every Christian is supposed to be an "evangelist" in the restricted sense of one who intentionally seeks out people who are not believers in order to share the gospel with them. That is a worthy and necessary ministry, but not every Christian has the gift for it (see Eph. 4:11–12). Virtually every Christian, however, lives and moves in a world of conversation and communication, a network of dialogue and decision making, where the distinctive way one sees the world is constantly coming to expression. It is here, in the give-and-take of workaday conversation, that Christian people need to find their voices.

We have already noted the widespread loss of such a voice, the kerygmatic laryngitis of contemporary Christians, and now we must acknowledge that at least part of this public silence among Christians comes not because they do not understand the radical character of the faith but, to the contrary, because they perceive it quite well.

At a deep level, most Christian people know that evangelism and ethics are bound together. One can only speak as a Christian when one lives as a Christian. There may be many reasons why Christian folk are reticent to speak openly of their faith to others. Sometimes they are simply embarrassed to do so, fearing that they will put others on the spot. Perhaps they are unskilled in theological talk, or maybe they don't want to appear merely pious. I would like to suggest a deeper reason: namely, that church people rightly understand, if only intuitively, that such belief statements are meaningless apart from lives that reflect the truth of those claims, and they hesitate to speak truths they fear their lives do not embody. In other words, because many Christians have serious doubts about how well they "walk the walk" (to use the language of the camp meeting), they are not comfortable "talking the talk." As ethicist Stanley Hauerwas has stated:

> The story of being a Christian involves claims on our lives which few of us feel able to avow we have fulfilled. Who among us feels free to affirm that we are or have been faithful disciples of the man who died on the cross? Who among us is able to say, much less live, what it means to claim that every moment of our lives should take the form of a thankful attitude to the God we believe is the beginning and end of our existence? Therefore, we are hesitant to claim our being "a Christian," as we know such a claim involves more than simply believing this or that about God, Jesus, or the world.[9]

The preacher must respect this attitude, not only because it is deeply felt but also because it grows out of an accurate perception of the evangelical task. Only those who live the Christian struggle in their lives have the power to articulate the Christian news in their speaking. Or, again in the words of Hauerwas, "The truth of the story we find in the gospels is known finally only through the kind of lives it produces. If such lives are absent then no amount of hermeneutical theory or manipulation can make those texts meaningful."[10] Put simply, then, we cannot send people out to be evangelists if the church from which they are sent is not engaged in passionate and costly Christian practice. Preachers who do not address ethical concerns forfeit their ability to address evangelistic concerns.

Another reason why Christian people are reticent about their faith in everyday settings is that they lack the necessary vocabulary. Without being romantically nostalgic about some golden past, we can acknowledge that there was a time when the common round of Christian folk possessed a basic theological and biblical vocabulary and knew, to some extent, how to use it. Words like grace, atonement, sin, and redemption were a more or less working vocabulary for people, at least church people, and they used them to make sense out of their lives. We speak often of biblical illiteracy, but even more pervasive is theological aphasia, the loss of theological speech. The biblical metaphors and theological categories have fallen away like the robes of royalty, and the vocabulary most readily at hand to describe ourselves, our world, and our deepest needs is the language of psychotherapy, or game playing, or human potential. The vocabulary of the faith, if employed at all, is used only to describe those experiences which are inward and private or conventionally religious. In other words, theological words are now not terms to be used to describe life; they have become words to be used to describe religion.

So what? What is lost when theological words drop away from ordinary discourse? A great deal, as a matter of fact. What is lost is the capacity to perceive and to tell the truth about the fullness of human life and finally the capacity to discern the holy in our midst. In other words, theological language is the only language we have to point to the presence of God-with-us. It cannot be replaced by any other language, and not to use this language is simply not to be able to say what is happening. Preaching that equips people for the ministry of evangelism will, in large measure, be dedicated to giving back to Christian people the theological vocabulary they need to speak the truth and to express the peculiar vision at the heart of the gospel.

An Example Text

The encounter between Jesus and the Samaritan woman (John 4:1–42) is a rich and multifaceted text, and one way to view it is as a paradigm of the activity of evangelism. The setting of the story, of course, is the old landmark, Jacob's well, where Jesus, wearied by his journey from Judea to Galilee, sat down alone to rest. The story gets going in earnest when the woman comes to the well to draw water.

Notice that Jesus begins the conversation with the woman by saying, "Give me a drink" (v. 7). This seemingly simple request is, however, not merely a breaking of the silence; it is also a daring assault upon the cultural barriers erected between Jew and Samaritan, man and woman. The good news, which will soon be spoken to her, is even at this point challenging the social foundations of the world in which she lives.

What follows is an exchange that takes place at two levels. The woman speaks the language of ordinary discourse; Jesus speaks the language of life in the eternal. They use the same words, but they are speaking two different languages. She speaks of water and thirst, and her reference is Jacob's well. Jesus speaks of water and thirst, and his reference is the Spirit. Those who hear the story are already aware of the invasion of one world by another. Finally she utters her ironic request, a sentence that hovers suspensefully between the two levels, that originates in one world but reaches toward the other: "Sir, give me this water, that I may not thirst, nor come here to draw" (v. 15).

Suddenly the conversation takes an unexpected turn as Jesus says, "Go, call your husband, and come here." She responds with the facts, but not the whole truth: "I have no husband" (vs. 16–17). Jesus' reply that she has had five husbands and is living with a man who is not her husband (v. 18) is often taken as an indication of the woman's ethical laxity, as if she were a reckless divorcée currently living in casual immorality. Surely, though, this is an anachronistic and misleading view. It is far more likely, given the social circumstances of the time, that instead of abandoning husbands she has been abandoned by them and is now with a man who will not afford her the dignity of marriage. Jesus is not naming her promiscuity, but rather her pain. The conversation has revealed her deepest predicament, to which the good news will not come as an abstraction but as a word of healing.

Recognizing now the changed environment, the claim upon her world, the woman begins, interestingly, to speak the language of theology, to talk of prophets and worship. Even so, her language is conventional; she repeats the religious slogans of her day, the clichés about the religious differences between Jews and Samaritans (vs. 19–20). What she says is the equivalent of a report on the religion page of *Time* or *Newsweek:* some religious groups believe this and some believe that; isn't that an interesting difference in religious groups! Jesus responds with theological language that opens up and redefines the situation, with words that expose the claim of God upon her and her world (vs. 22–24).

Wondrously, she finds her own voice, haltingly and uncertainly, beginning to speak this new language: "I know that Messiah is coming (he who is called Christ); when he comes, he will show us all things" (v. 25). And then comes the moment, the gospel, the word, the good news: "I who speak to you am he" (v. 26). The One who breaks down the walls of hostility, the One who discerns her deepest need, the One who stands with her in her pain, the One whose word opens up the future and who calls her to worship in spirit and truth is none other than God in Jesus Christ. She hears Jesus' words as *news,* good news, that must be told to others as invitation and promise (vs. 29, 39).

Notes

1. John H. Leith, *The Reformed Imperative: What the Church Has to Say That No One Else Can Say* (Philadelphia: Westminster Press, 1988), p. 42.

2. D. T. Niles, as quoted in Gabriel Fackre, *Word in Deed: Theological Themes in Evangelism* (Grand Rapids: Wm. B. Eerdmans Publishing Co., 1975), p. 26.

3. George A. Lindbeck, *The Nature of Doctrine: Religion and Theology in a Postliberal Age* (Philadelphia: Westminster Press, 1984), p. 132.

4. Ibid.

5. Carl Michaelson, "On the Gospel," in Richard Lischer, ed., *Theories of Preaching: Selected Readings in the Homiletical Tradition* (Durham, N.C.: Labyrinth Press, 1987), pp. 32–33.

6. William Muehl, *Why Preach? Why Listen?* (Philadelphia: Fortress Press, 1986), p. 11.

7. Walker Percy, *The Message in the Bottle* (New York: Farrar, Straus & Giroux, 1975), p. 114.

8. Ibid., pp. 114–116.

9. Stanley Hauerwas, *Christian Existence Today: Essays on Church, World, and Living In Between* (Durham, N.C.: Labyrinth Press, 1988), pp. 39–40.

10. Ibid., pp. 40–41.

7

Preaching About
The Ecumenical Church—
Beyond the Melting Pot

Charles L. Rice

As this century was beginning, Josiah Royce, the philosopher, expressed his uneasiness about the American melting pot, that if we continued in that homogenizing direction we would "approach a dead level of harassed mediocrity."[1] That forecast is not far from what has actually happened in our culture, and it could as well be a description of many of our efforts at ecumenical worship. Who among us would rate the typical Wednesday evening Thanksgiving service, baccalaureate, or the interchurch event high among liturgical experiences?

Ordinarily these events are centered on preaching, with a secondary emphasis on musical performance and a sometimes heroic effort to fit in all the clergy in the town, who take various parts in what often turns out to be a jack-in-the-box affair. But the sermon is usually the primary thing. How might we approach the ecumenical event as preachers? How are we to understand such an event, what would be the preacher's aim, and what resources in scripture, liturgy, and theology come to hand?

Were we to go beyond Royce's dire prediction to his prescription, we would try to keep a clear sense of the church—indeed, of our particular communions. Royce thought that the way to connect with other cultures, even strange ones, was to cultivate real appreciation for one's own heritage. "Loyalty to loyalty," as he called this larger commitment to humankind, was learned by real devotion to one's own people and folk-ways, by way of an enlightened provincialism. For this reason he urged against the melting pot, which could only dissolve the individual's sense of people and place that, he believed, fostered mutual respect among diverse peoples.

Local and Catholic Preaching

If preaching is organic to specific sacramental communities, as virtually everyone who thinks about homiletics would as-sert,[2] then the preacher who steps outside the pastoral and priestly situation had better do so quite intentionally and re-flectively. Preaching belongs more appropriately to the local than to the catholic church, though in each sermon most preachers would wish to represent both. Hans Küng refers to the catholic church as "the total church," and says that each local congregation "represents and realizes" the total, catholic church.[3] It is this situation which we see on the ecumenical occasion, that preaching is somewhat displaced from its proper ground, but at the same time on friendly territory. Preaching on such an occasion is a contribution to the cath-olicity of the local church. Küng writes:

> A Church does not become uncatholic by being limited to a local church, but by being a limited local church which has cut itself off from other Churches and hence from the whole, entire Church, by concentrating solely on its own life and faith and trying to be self-sufficient.[4]

Anyone who preaches knows this to be true, and important. We preach as pastors, among people with names and ad-dresses, but that is not, finally, the full ambit of preaching. Every sermon includes within its range the catholic church, and when it does not, both preacher and preaching suffer from an overweening provincialism. The old lawyer in the play *In-herit the Wind* tells the young schoolteacher, pilloried by a small-town mentality, that Christianity is not necessarily what goes on in that town. In all its seasons, preaching is both local and catholic. So the preacher called upon to speak to the wider church is, in doing so, acknowledging an ecumenicity that is always the context of preaching, however parochial a given Sunday morning might be.

The sticky wicket is that virtually all our ecumenical events center on the preacher. That is increasingly problematic in a pluralistic society. We have come a long way from the homogeneous days of the Puritans when preaching could actually function as a kind of "social sacrament," a whole society cohering around this weekly eloquence. And we have come even further from the locus of unity in the early church. Despite difference in opinion and practice, says Küng, the early church achieved a sacramental unity. These early churches, while divided into different factions, were in communion with one another.

> The early Church is a community of Churches which are united in acknowledging the one Lord Jesus Christ and which are distinct from all those who do not confess the one Lord; they are all united in the communion of the sacred meal through one and the same baptism.[5]

We have the fact to face that in the ecumenical event, as in the weekly worship of many of our churches, preaching may be called upon to bear more freight than it can carry, as diversity tries to find unity around the pulpit. That might be more easily achieved around the Holy Table, which, despite repeated efforts in the history of the church to make it so, is not so dependent upon consensus on either doctrinal or social norms. It may well be that a growing pluralism will lead us toward an increasingly eucharistic unity.

But when we turn our attention, given the ethos of most of our churches and communities, to preaching in an ecumenical setting, we recognize that an undue burden may be placed on the preacher at such an occasion. Anyone who has preached at the Thanksgiving Eve service or an interdenominational rally, not to mention such an observance of civil religion as a baccalaureate, will probably agree that there is more to carry here than preaching will comfortably bear.

The first question, of course, is whether or not to follow the lectionary. Some would say that the ecumenical service is the ideal time to depart from that, to try to read the community or to find a text especially appropriate to promoting unity (which is probably an agenda to avoid, since we may assume the unity of baptized Christians; the church *is* one). If the occasion were prompted by a crisis or a particular need—either to mourn or to celebrate—then the free choice of readings from scripture might be indicated. On the other hand, many would say that one of the most significant ecumenical achievements in this half of the century is the common lectionary. Lay people and clergy alike are gaining ownership of these common pericopes to the degree that the scriptures have their own life in the congregation's worship, quite apart from the preacher's choice and use of texts. If that is the case, then to forgo the lectionary on an ecumenical occasion should be done only on reflection. Aside from the daily lectionary provided by some of our churches, there will often be no lectionary for the occasions of ecumenical worship. But the preacher ought at least to consider the readings for the preceding Sunday: reading those lessons and preaching on one of them would forge an immediate link with many who had heard them read the previous Sunday. It is a way of giving the feeling that we are, despite our differences, "singing out of the same hymnbook."

The Resources of Scripture and Tradition

At the same time, the special occasion does provide an opportunity to locate the concerns that unite us as Christians—even as citizens of town, nation, and the world—and to bring to bear the resources of scripture and tradition in a way that addresses the common aspirations and problems of our "global village," to use the language of Marshall McLuhan. The priorities of the World Council of Churches that have issued from the Vancouver Assembly, one of the great ecumenical events of our time, might serve as a guide for our preaching at the extra-parish event. The World Council has been promoting since 1987 its program of peace, justice, and the integrity of creation. The call is to locate, in the church and in the world, the places where Christ is present among us, where the Spirit is at work in the world, and to determine how we shall live on the earth with all living things.[6] Let us consider this as a place to begin, whether preparing to preach on World Day of Prayer, at a community service for Memorial Day, or in an ecumenical Lenten series.

Peace. Few people, of whatever denomination, would not give this top priority. Merely coming to an ecumenical gathering is probably a move toward reconciliation and shalom. The preacher at such an event is in a good place to speak of peace and to do so in connection with the confession of the hoped-for reign of God common to Christians and to Jews as well. Here we may preach Christ as the one who breaks down the dividing walls (Ephesians), who does not recognize the conventional divisions among persons, races, and nations (the parables, the Sermon on the Mount), and at whose gracious table all are welcome. It would not be amiss to preach on the Eucharist as that event in which, under the signs of suffering and death, in the face of enmity and betrayal, the healing and reconciling love of God is seen. We hear the call to be reconciled to our sisters and brothers as we approach this table, a call we must hear as possibility more than legalistic requirement. With this table in view, the inviting Christ offering forgiveness and reconciliation to all, we can find the way of peace.

Ideally, our ecumenical gatherings would be at the Eucharist. Recognizing our common baptism—as virtually all Christians do, regardless of the baptismal form—we would gather at one table to share the presence of Christ. Since that is not the case, much to our loss, the Eucharist continues to be for the ecumenical church not a reconciling sacrament but a divisive doctrine. The preacher could use her or his time to lift up Holy Communion as the primary event in which Christ breaks down walls and calls us to meet at a basic, human level. Can we make too much of this, that we claim to know the peace-giving presence of Christ as we eat and drink together? Is not that the quintessential ecumenism, and must we not say that wherever people are able to come from east and west, south and north, and sit down at table, Christ is present there? Does not preaching need to make more of this, particularly since the many churches tend to displace the Eucharist by preaching?

Taizé, the ecumenical community in central France, is devoted to overcoming the ancient rivalries of Europe as well as the split between Catholic and Protestant. How the community does that can be known only by going there, but some features of Taizé's life are pertinent here. People of all ages, languages, and communions camp out in the hills of Burgundy, eat simple food, and pray together three times a day, beginning each day with the Eucharist. The scriptures are read and the prayers said in several tongues at each service, a practice which, far from being disconcerting, achieves what Royce hoped for, an awareness of the other which can lead to real community. For us, the guidance of Taizé would be toward leading people into new awareness of communion in Christ that transcends our doctrinal differences and even our preaching. This peace for which the broken church longs can be served as the preacher reminds the people of baptism and points toward Communion as the focal point of Christ's reconciling presence in the world.

Justice. Taizé, which greatly influenced the Vancouver Assembly, holds together peace and justice: it is the Christian's participation in God's gracious reign in Christ that impels and sustains our work. The motive power for locating the Spirit's action and joining it is the foretaste of God's new age which we know in Jesus Christ, especially in the community of word and sacrament. How then would the preacher advocate action for justice in the ecumenical assembly?

If the preacher begins with the occasion *liturgically*—that is, with the intention of making this the people's event—then we might choose among three ways to go: to follow the lectionary, to isolate and address an issue that the diverse congregation has in common, or to locate a truly common text. In some cases the second option is dictated by the occasion; there has been a great loss, or some momentous event is calling for the community's attention. There will be little question on those occasions as to what the preacher should talk about, and sometimes, as at the death of Martin Luther King, Jr., the texts will be supplied as well. But most ecumenical occasions that occur outside the ordinary cycle of Sundays and holy days afford the opportunity to preach on one of the texts that almost any

Christian would recognize as belonging in some special sense to the ecumenical church.

For example, one of our common texts is the Lord's Prayer, the one prayer said by all Christians. To choose such a text serves, from the outset, to deliver the service into the hands of the people. This prayer of Jesus belongs—perhaps more than any other—to every Christian, an ownership that would be tacitly recognized by the entire ecumenical congregation. Such a text rescues the preacher from having to carry too much weight—having to be novel, to come up with an interesting idea—and calls the congregation into ownership of scripture and liturgy. A pastor said to me recently, "I am feeling the freedom of ordinariness, that I don't have to come up with something new every Sunday." The tendency in preparing for the ecumenical occasion will be to "fall back into a yoke of bondage," to make a heroic effort to do something special. Preaching from an ordinary common text is one way to avoid this and to find in what everybody already owns a liberating source for preaching.

Consider the Lord's Prayer as an ideal, even paradigmatic, pericope for connecting with an ecumenical congregation, calling them to ownership of the liturgy, and moving them toward action for social justice. The idea is to communicate right away that this prayer, which Jesus taught, belongs to each of us without distinction. Having established this, the preacher can then proceed to fresh exegesis and contemporary application which shows that much of the tradition we share remains to be appropriated and applied to our common life. In the prayer, the opening acclamation is the reason for our being here, to hallow God's name, and the first and second petitions are as closely linked to that intention as to the petitions that follow. This prayer delivers us from narrowness and parochialism—whoever hallows God's name shares our liturgy—and from the individualism and sectarianism that plague us. We pray for daily bread, for the forgiveness of our sins, to be saved from evil: not for some narrow agenda preoccupied with our individual salvation or the success and comfort of our group but for one purpose, that God's will may be done, God's reign come on earth to the full.[7] This is a prayer for the new age which has come in Jesus, which we know in baptism and Eucharist, and for whose fruition we pray and work. It is possible, as James Breech believes,[8] that this prayer comes from the setting of Jesus' table fellowship, the origin of the Eucharist. In any case, the ambiguous *epiousion,* which might be translated either "daily" or "for the future," suggests what we experience in the Eucharist, that daily bread and eschatological food cannot finally be distinguished. That is where all Christians live, asking for daily bread while living gratefully, in remembrance of Jesus, toward the future.

So, in this familiar prayer, the essential elements of ecumenical Christianity come into view. Though there may not be another text that is so clearly held in common by the catholic church, others to consider include such familiar parables as the Good Samaritan or the prodigal son. In each case, the preacher once more has the opportunity to move beyond conventional interpretation, and in a way that opens easily toward the ecumenical occasion. Long before Luke 10:30–37 was a call to dutiful neighborliness (too often the tone of ecumenism!) it was a picture of radical freedom to cross over conventional lines and be available to the stranger.[9] The story of the prodigal also, to quote John Crossan, announces God as "the shatterer" of the familiar, conventional world in which people are divided, rather than united, by moral opinion and religious observance. See James Breech's discussion of the parable as a story that enables us to celebrate together both the actual world and the grace of God, while recognizing our differences and being aware of the distinctly "other."[10] These two parables are ecumenical both in their usage in the church and in the thrust of their message.

What other texts hold a similar place in the church's life and worship? Perhaps the preacher should choose a pericope that is part of the eucharistic liturgy, perhaps 1 Corinthians 11 or one of the texts on baptism, Romans 6 or Ephesians 4. There are also some vivid pictures of the early church as a community of word and sacrament that lend themselves as common texts of the ecumenical church, especially Acts 2 and Colossians 2. Or one could preach on what we mean by the word of God, paying attention, once more, to the common terrain of scripture and preaching. The liturgical tradition, including prayers, creeds, and the rich lode of hymnody, should be considered also when seeking material or even primary texts for preaching.

This is not to lead the preacher away from the World Council's second priority, seeking out those places in the world where the Spirit of God is at work for justice. On the contrary, if our most common text, the Lord's Prayer, were our guide, our liturgy would never be far from politics. We come to the Eucharist, seek to live out the meaning of our baptism, and give ourselves to the catholic church in the hope of God's will being done on earth as it is in heaven, that what we experience of Christ present in the church might be manifest in politics, economics, and the whole social order. Using the ecumenical occasion to say this clearly is a great opportunity for the preacher, and the occasion itself—which calls us away from merely parochial concerns—can reinforce this message. Could the preacher lead us, on an ecumenical occasion, to see with fresh eyes that the story of the Good Samaritan is a liberating narrative of the breaking in of God's reign on earth?

The preacher might also turn to a story that evokes our common humanity. This could come from the arts, the media, or the local setting. I recall a folk mass at the Cathedral of San Fernando, in San Antonio, Texas, attended by people of many denominations. The priest in charge of that parish told the story of his people, how many are displaced persons who do not speak English and are without legal status. He began the service, standing at the holy table with the parish's mariachi band—which had been playing for some time while waiting for him to arrive—arrayed behind him, by telling us that he had been detained at the hospital. A young man riding a freight train out of Mexico had caught his leg in the boxcar coupling and it had been amputated. The telling of that story became the context for all that happened in the service, and everyone who came to the Communion table carried the human drama along. Such a story—it need not be so dramatic—can galvanize a community, making people hungry for prayer and sharing in the communion of Christ. The preacher at an ecumenical gathering will certainly want to be alert to the human story—

from the very town, or from the media or arts—which involves us simply because we are human. Then, having found and told that story, the preacher will need to employ his or her own art in connecting it with the Story which brings us together in the sharing of word and sacrament.

The integrity of creation. The theologian who provides a perspective for preaching on this theme is Matthew Fox.[11] He calls the church to "creation spirituality," to move away from the dualism and patterns of domination that contribute to the present ecological crisis. Christ is the one who unites us with earth and all that lives, and to live in Christ is to enter more and more into the goodness of creation. We have been too prone, especially in preaching, to emphasize the realm of redemption to the neglect of creation. The result is scattered upon a landscape that reveals the limited definition we have given to Christ's salvation. One could build a valuable sermon simply by connecting the words "ecumenical" and "earth"; the preacher could simply begin by reminding the congregation that *oikoumenē* means "the inhabited world" of faithful people among whom, as Paul hoped, the word of Christ might richly dwell.

Two powerful ideas for sermons come to mind along this line. Peter Fribley, pastor of the Presbyterian Church in Oskaloosa, Iowa, once asked a group of theologians to consider the question: If we do eventually destroy the inhabited earth with nuclear weapons, would the purposes of God in Jesus Christ be thwarted? That question, however one answers it, puts in sharp relief the issue of the relation between creation and redemption. Again, Professor Paul Wilson, of Emmanuel College in Toronto, built a sermon around what he called two of the primary—and we might add, ecumenical—images of our time, the missiles being launched from their silos and the earth as a small blue ball floating in space, as seen from the moon. In that juxtaposition, the beauty and peace of the created order and the threat to God's creation posed by human sin, the call of the gospel to both thanksgiving and action was clear. These ideas and images pose the crucial questions of the integrity of creation in relation to the gospel of Christ.

Consider also the ready connection between primary Christian symbols and the ecological problems we face. A pastor groans that she must baptize children with polluted water, even as the fisherman watches acid rain kill the lake which he and his family have enjoyed for generations. The air, breath of life which all living things share and for both Jews and Christians the most common metaphor for the Spirit of God, becomes more and more carcinogenic. Now even the dimensions and colors of the Grand Canyon cannot be seen on many days of the year. The human body is dishonored by racism, sexism, drugs, and consumerism, not to mention hunger. In many parts of the world, daily bread is not there, and in other places where there is plenty, honest bread (like pure food) is hard to come by, so that for the affluent and overfed "daily bread," like "body of Christ," becomes an eroded metaphor. Some are too hungry to hear the message; many, too full and overstimulated to hunger for the bread of life. Plants and animals, for which we are given stewardship, diminish and suffer throughout the world while mountains of human garbage grow. The people who come to worship with their brothers and sisters of other communions live together in this world, directly affected in their bodies by the realities of our life on earth; this gives a second meaning to the word "ecumenical." And all these concerns connect, when imaginatively considered, with the earthy metaphors of sacramental Christianity, giving the preacher an extraordinary opportunity to preach the gospel as the redemption of the *world,* as the purpose of God to achieve the wholeness of creation.

Finally, all of this would be advanced by making the event as liturgical as possible: that is, by making it the work of the people. The tendency on these occasions is toward clericalism, lining up a preacher with the other clergy as backup. The people's liturgy, by means of bidding prayers, lay readers, and more hymn singing than performed music, should be the aim. There is something distinctly less than ecumenical about the service in which people are largely spectators, especially when there is no celebration of the Eucharist. At the ecumenical occasion, especially, it may take a special effort to make the event an experience of interaction, beauty, shared concerns,

common texts, and corporate prayer. This does not mean
having a cast of dozens getting up front and doing things.
Some of the most participatory liturgies are presided over by
one person. It probably does mean a sermon of modest pro-
portions; as a rule of thumb, the bigger the occasion, the
smaller the sermon, both as to material and length. In many
cases there will be—in the absence of Holy Communion this
becomes especially important—a social hour following. This
means that in preaching on the ecumenical occasion, for the
purposes of focusing and of allowing time for both liturgical
participation and social intercourse, less is definitely more.

In his book *Wine Talk,* Frank Prial writes about "the best
bottle I ever had." He concludes that most often that accolade
is not so much for the vintage as for the occasion: "The people
and the talk made the wine what it was."[12] Could not the same
be said of preaching at its best? It must be what we hope for
each Sunday, and especially on those occasions when we have
the privilege of preaching the gospel to a more variegated mix
of faithful people, among whom, as Paul hoped, the word of
Christ might dwell richly (Col. 3:16).

Notes

1. "Provincialism," in *The Social Philosophy of Josiah Royce,* ed.
Stuart G. Brown (Syracuse, N.Y.: Syracuse University Press,
1950), p. 56.

2. For the best statement on this, see Joseph Sittler, *The
Anguish of Preaching* (Philadelphia: Fortress Press, 1966), especially ch. 1.

3. Hans Küng, *The Church* (Garden City, N.Y.: Doubleday &
Co., 1976), p. 388.

4. Ibid.

5. Ibid., p. 382.

6. Preman Niles, *Resisting the Threats to Life: Covenanting for
Justice, Peace, and the Integrity of Creation* (Geneva: World Council
of Churches Publications, 1989), along with a series of seven
World Council of Churches resource packets, *Justice, Peace,
and the Integrity of Creation,* would be the sources for further
information.

7. A very helpful resource on this common text is Charles Talbert's commentary on Luke, *Reading Luke: A Literary and Theological Commentary on the Third Gospel* (New York: Crossroad Publishing Co., 1982).

8. James Breech, *The Silence of Jesus* (Philadelphia: Fortress Press, 1983), pp. 53ff.

9. See especially the commentaries of John D. Crossan, *In Parables* (New York: Harper & Row, 1973), and Robert W. Funk, *Language, Hermeneutic, and Word of God* (New York: Harper & Row, 1966).

10. Breech, *The Silence of Jesus,* pp. 184–212.

11. Matthew Fox, *Original Blessing: A Primer in Creation Spirituality* (Sante Fe, N. Mex.: Bear & Co., 1983) and his *The Coming of the Cosmic Christ* (New York: Harper & Row, 1988).

12. Frank J. Prial, *Wine Talk* (New York: Times Books, 1978), p. 7.

8

Preaching About Stewardship—
Koinōnia and the Christian
Relationship with Resources

Ronald J. Allen

Among Christians today, stewardship is often popularly understood as a code word for dealing with money in the church.[1] The primary assignments of the congregation's stewardship committee are to raise the annual budget and to manage the congregation's finances. Stewardship is functionally understood as one activity in the church's life that takes place alongside other activities. In this way of approaching stewardship, the preacher typically focuses stewardship sermons on such matters as the Christian understanding and use of money.

In relatively recent years, the idea of Christian stewardship has been expanded to include the Christian use of all of life's resources. Stewardship is not one activity alongside others in the Christian life and community but is what we do with all that we have and all that we are. The Christian steward is concerned with the use of money, time, ability, social relationship, and the natural environment. Douglas John Hall captures this expansive view of contemporary stewardship in the title of his book *Christian Mission: The Stewardship of Life in the Kingdom of Death.*[2]

We have become increasingly aware of the importance of language in human life. The words we use to name and describe the world help shape our perception of the world and help order our behavior in it.[3] The Christian use of the words "steward" and "stewardship" is derived from the biblical picture of the steward. Critical reflection upon the biblical image of the steward reveals that this image is problematic as a way for the Christian community to speak of its relationship to God, and to the social and natural realms. Indeed, the biblical picture of the steward works against many of the very things which the modern interpreters of stewardship wish to encourage.

In this chapter, I will point to difficulties posed by the steward image. I will then posit Paul's understanding of *koinōnia* as an appropriate, credible, and timely metaphor by which preachers may speak of the Christian relationship to others, both personal and material.[4]

The Image of Stewardship Reexamined

The steward was a familiar figure in the everyday world of the Bible. In the Hebrew Bible, the steward was a person who was in charge of the household affairs and/or the business matters of a master and owner (e.g., Gen. 43:16–25; 44:1–13).[5]

The same idea is found in the Septuagint (the translation of the Hebrew Bible into Greek and the form of the Jewish scriptures typically used by the early church). In the Septuagint, the Greek word *oikonomos* (steward) is used for the household and business administrator responsible to the owner;[6] the word *oikonomia* (stewardship) refers to the activity of a steward[7] and to the realm for which a monarch is responsible.[8]

As far as I can tell, the steward word group is not used in the Hebrew Bible to describe the human responsibility to "manage" the world or its affairs before God. And in the Septuagint, such a designation is found only in Numbers 12:7–8. The steward metaphor, then, can hardly be regarded as a staple of the Hebrew way of thinking about the place and responsibility of human beings in the world.

The biblical texts that most fully inform the Christian image of stewardship are a very small number of parables found in Luke and Matthew. The stewardship parables often unfold along the following lines:

1. A householder or estate owner goes away on a trip.

2. A steward is left in charge of the household or estate.

3. The householder returns and conducts what we might call a performance evaluation of the work of the steward during the householder's absence.

4. The householder rewards—or punishes—the steward according to the quality of the steward's performance.

In this scheme, humankind is similar to the steward while God is similar to the owner.[9]

This is the case in Luke 12:41–48. The master sets the steward over the household with the specific instruction to give the members of the household their food at the right time (v. 42). The master points out that the steward who faithfully performs this task will be blessed by being set over all the master's possessions (vs. 43–44). The servant who is neglectful of his responsibility, who is abusive, or who gets drunk, will be punished at the time of the master's return and will be excommunicated (vs. 45–46). The servant who knew what the master expected but did not act on it will "receive a severe beating" (v. 47). The servant who did not know what the master required and then "did what deserved a beating, shall receive a light beating" (v. 48). This story, which might be called the parable of the condemned and beaten stewards, is told to demonstrate the importance of being ready when Jesus returns in glory and judgment (v. 40). The parable of the talents (Matt. 25:14–30; Luke 19:12–27) is similar.[10]

In these stories, the servants have great responsibility and accountability but no ownership of the things for which they are accountable. Their relationship with the owner is strictly a matter of accounting, and in one case the master is even described as "hard" (Matt. 25:24). This latter owner's standard of performance is hardly attainable by the typical servant, for this owner reaps without sowing and gathers without winnowing (v. 24)!

To be sure, the contemporary use of the notion of stewardship is not limited to the particular nuances highlighted here. Nonetheless, even when images are taken up, reinterpreted, and transported from one milieu to another, they seldom lose all their baggage. The root development of the metaphor of stewardship has five problems that diminish its utility for the church of today.

First, by using the landowner-steward relationship as an analogy for the relationship between God and humankind, the stewardship model suggests that God is removed from the world and from the work of the steward. In the stewardship parables, the owner is often an absentee landlord who assigns responsibility, disappears while the responsibility is carried out, and then returns to judge the steward on the degree to which the steward has successfully carried out the assignment in the owner's absence. To be sure, the parables should not be treated as allegories in which we assume that the estate holder *is* God. But, as a way of thinking analogically about God's relationship with the world, the model of the absentee landowner runs directly counter to one of the central affirmations of the gospel: namely, that God is always present with and involved in the affairs of creation.[11]

Second, the stewardship metaphor can distort our understanding of the nature of God. The heart of the Christian confession is that God is pure, unbounded love. But in the stewardship parables, the landowner is typically represented as hard and demanding, without compassion or mercy.

Third, the steward metaphor comes very close to advocating works righteousness. The stewards earn the acceptance and approval of the owner on the basis of their performance. The stewards who do not prove themselves worthy receive punishment.

Fourth, the stewardship paradigm establishes a negative tone in the human relationship with God. The stewards must always worry about whether their performance is satisfactory.

Fifth, the stewardship model can foster individualism and can even discourage the steward from entering into a positive relationship of community with others. The hierarchical stewardship paradigm may be diagrammed as follows:

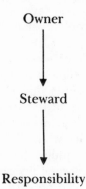

Owner

Steward

Responsibility

(persons, goods, land, business)

Indeed, the steward acts autonomously in ways that will improve *the treatment of the steward by the owner.* The stewardship paradigm thereby frustrates the yearnings for community and for mutual, egalitarian relationships that are important in our time.[12]

The Bible itself suggests another metaphor that is more appropriate to the gospel and is better suited to our time than the steward. This is the Pauline notion of *koinōnia.*

Paul's Use of *Koinōnia* as an Image for Preaching on the Christian Relationship with Resources

The *koinōnia* word group in the Pauline corpus is often translated into English by the language of "fellowship." In contemporary North America, "to have fellowship" typically means to have a warm, positive feeling toward another. But in the world of the first century, *koinōnia* had a much stronger and more dynamic meaning.

For many years, scholars have noticed that *koinōnia* and its cognates were prominent in commercial circles in the first century to describe a business partner. This use is found, for instance, in the Gospel of Luke, where James and John are described as partners with Simon in the fishing business (Luke 5:10). In the business sector, to be a *koinōnos* (partner) was to be joined together in a legal relationship much as business partners are related today.

The *koinōnia* word family was used in the ancient world to speak of relationships outside the world of business as well, but even here the stress is upon mutual commitment to a project or to the completion of a task.[13] This dimension of the meaning of *koinōnia* is suggested by the English words "participation" or "partnership," which are sometimes used to translate *koinōnia*.

Even more specifically, J. Paul Sampley has noticed that *koinōnia* was used in the Hellenistic era to name social contracts among people. A *koinōnia* was a "consortium made up of persons who were drawn together by some mutually valued goal or purpose."[14] A *koinōnia* could be established in one of four ways: (1) by mandate, (2) by permanent sale of something (or someone), (3) by temporary hire of something (or someone), (4) by the *voluntary* association of one person with others.

A *koinōnia* could be established on the basis of "nothing more than the agreement of the parties," and it "required neither witnesses nor written documents nor notification of authorities." A partnership "operated when partners agreed to use property or labor in common towards a particular goal that was beyond the property or labor itself."[15] Each partner contributed something to the endeavor (e.g., property, labor, skill, status), and "no matter what one contributed to the partnership, one was to share in whatever profits or losses" accrued. The foundation of the *koinōnia* was "mutual trust and reciprocity."[16]

"The good of all the partners must be served by the actions of the individual partner *(socius).*"[17] The partnership community existed as long as the members were committed to pursue the good which led them to enter into the *koinōnia*. One of the partners could act in behalf of the whole community provided that the partner's actions were in accord with the good of the community. The *koinōnia* depended largely upon "a strong sense of obligation to keep one's word," a trait especially valued in the Hellenistic age.[18]

In several passages, Paul describes the church as a *koinōnia*. This suggests that Paul understood the church as a partnership in which each of the partners was joined to the other (and to the community) in the service of the common goal of bearing witness to the gospel. Several of these passages are suggestive for Christian preaching on the Christian relationship with others.

In Galatians 2:1–10, Paul interprets the relationship between his mission to the Gentiles and the mission of the Jerusalem church to the Jewish people. Verse 9 is key: "And when they perceived the grace that was given to me, James and Cephas and John, who were reputed to be pillars, gave to me and Barnabas the right hand of fellowship, that we should go to the Gentiles and they to the circumcised." The giving of the right hand of fellowship *(dexias koinōnias)* was an act that formalized a Hellenistic voluntary association in the Hellenistic world.[19] Verse 10 notes that a part of the Gentile share in the partnership was to give money for the poor: that is, the impoverished.

Neither the Jerusalem community nor the Pauline mission bears the whole responsibility for the Christian witness, but in doing its part each sector is fulfilling its responsibility to the whole. Furthermore, the collection of money by the Gentile churches for the poor is not simply a donation but represents a part of the Gentile share in the partnership.

Second Corinthians 8 and 9 is Paul's most sustained discussion of the collection and its meaning.[20] The Corinthians, evidently, have been slow to raise money for the church in Jerusalem, and Paul writes to encourage them to fulfill their part in the partnership. Throughout these two chapters, Paul uses language that presumes the Corinthians are in a relationship of *koinōnia* with the Jerusalem congregation (see 8:4, 6, 8, 10–14, esp. 14, 24; 9:5). The giving of money is thus a way of saying "yes!" to the continuation of the partnership. According to 9:12–13, the "contribution" (which translates *koinōnia* in 9:13) ultimately "not only supplies the wants of the saints but also overflows in many thanksgivings to God." The collection is thus a significant means whereby the Corinthians meet human need, declare their solidarity with the Christians in Jerusalem, and give glory to God.

In 1 Corinthians 1:9, Paul declares that "God is faithful, by whom you were called into the fellowship *(koinōnia)* of his Son, Jesus Christ our Lord." The living Jesus is thus a living member of the partnership, albeit a very senior partner.[21]

A similar theme appears in Paul's discussion of the Corinthian practice of eating food that has been offered to idols in 1 Corinthians 10:14–22. Partaking of the Lord's Supper is "participation" *(koinōnia)* in the blood and body of Christ (v. 16), whereas those who eat the food that is offered to idols become "partners *(koinōnoi)* with demons" (v. 20). For Paul, then, the eating of a sacred meal bespeaks partnership, and Paul cautions the Corinthians to be wary of those with whom they enter into mutual commitment.

The eating of food offered to idols is no longer a direct problem for Christians, but, thinking analogously, the preacher might ask, What are some contemporary actions that bring us functionally into league with values and practices which, like the demons of Paul's day, are antithetical to the gospel? For instance, does the way we use our money bring us into functional partnership with business and governmental practices that are contrary to the gospel?

"I thank my God in all my remembrance of you," Paul begins Philippians, ". . . thankful for your partnership *(koinōnia)* in the gospel from the first day until now" (Phil. 1:3, 5). In an extraordinary passage, the apostle urges the Philippians to be "of the same mind" (2:2). This phrase, "to be of the same mind," is technical language that describes the partners in a *koinōnia.* [22] In this context, it refers to the partnership which the Philippians have been given in Christ Jesus (2:5–11). In this partnership, the Philippian Christians do their part by emptying themselves for one another (2:1–4, 14–16). By contrast the human tendency is to shore up oneself for the sake of self-preservation. But now, the grace of God as revealed in Christ provides the security and self-understanding that makes it possible for the Philippians to be self-emptying.

Commentators have long described Philippians 4:10–20 as a "receipt," written in formal commercial terminology, which Paul issues to the congregation because he has received their financial contributions in support of his ministry and which is thereby a typical *partnership* transaction (v. 15). But Paul moves beyond the commercial level in verses 18–20 to claim that the Philippian offering is "a sacrifice acceptable and pleasing to God." Furthermore, Paul claims in verse 19 that God will supply the need of the Philippians. Thus, "a mundane contractual performance by the Philippians towards Paul" is a mirror of the abundance of God's care.[23] The preacher might well help the congregation think about its use of its own resources as being such a mirror in the world of today. Indeed, this becomes a plumb line which the congregation can hang beside every aspect of its life: Does this act (this expenditure, this use of human energy or environmental material or whatever) witness to God's care for all the world?

The little book of Philemon is a clear example of the boldness that is possible in the bonds of the Christian *koinōnia*.[24] Paul assumes that Philemon is established in the *koinōnia* through faith (vs. 4–6). On the basis of this relationship, Paul appeals straightforwardly to Philemon as a partner (*koinōnos*, v. 17) to receive the runaway slave Onesimus back into Philemon's home and service even as Philemon would receive Paul. We moderns rightly regret that Paul did not ask for the slave to be freed. Nonetheless, the point is bracing: in *koinōnia* in Christ, Christians can make claims upon one another, even claims that involve material goods.

In Romans 15:22–29, Paul states that his immediate purpose is to take the collection *(koinōnia)* for the saints to Jerusalem (vs. 25–26). Verse 27 then places this simple action in an eschatological frame of reference: The Gentile Christians of Macedonia and Achaia are sending their material wealth to the Christians in Jerusalem. The eschatological theme is triggered by the reference to the Gentiles. In Isaiah's vision of the eschatological age, the Gentiles bring their wealth to God in Jerusalem (Isa. 60:1–7, esp. 5–7). Thus, when the Christians (who through Christ have come to share in the blessings of the God of the Jewish people) send their money to Jerusalem, that act is an eschatological sign. Probably few Christians today think of dropping their checks in the offering plate as acts of eschatological witness, and a preacher might greatly encourage the members of the congregation by helping them see the offering in that perspective.

Clark M. Williamson notices that "this *koinonial* web is much larger than what we usually call the church."

> Our impact on others, including ourselves in the future, is vast; the money I did not send to the United Negro College Fund is

just as important as what I sent to the Division of Higher Education, perhaps more so. The work a laywoman does, day by day, of preserving the structures of justice and liberty in the society is perhaps more important than any committee work at the church. The concern for developing a just society in all corners of the earth, in a way that either recognizes the rights of nature or is at least concerned to preserve the planet's ability to sustain life is an imperative concern. . . . The *koinonial* reality is vast.[25]

In this vast concern, the church witnesses to God's purpose for the whole of creation and embodies that purpose in the *koinōnia* of church life.

The image of *koinōnia,* then, is a wonderful lens for our perception of the Christian relationship to human and nonhuman others. We can note six particular strengths in this way of thinking.

First, the character and purposes of God are portrayed in a very positive way. God is the gracious initiator of the *koinōnia.* No longer an absentee landlord, God is constantly involved in the partnership.

Second, the members of the *koinōnia* are directly related to God, with one another and with the environment. The interrelatedness of those in the *koinōnia* may be represented by a web. The use of our resources thus becomes a way of giving expression to our mutuality.

Third, those committed to the *koinōnia* are accountable to one another and to God on a day-to-day basis in a context that receives its character from the God who is pure, unbounded love. The members are accountable for doing their part in the *koinōnia* and are mindful that failure to do so means harm to the other members and to the *koinōnia*'s purpose and goal. But because the *koinōnia* is centered in a gracious God, the failure to live up to the partnership does not mean being cast into outer darkness but does mean the importance of honestly recognizing one's failure and then recognizing that one has already been given the strength to do one's part.

Fourth, the partnership metaphor embraces the diversity within the Christian community. All Christians have something to contribute to the *koinōnia* and come together as equal partners in the gospel. To take a simple example, wealthy

Christians in the United States may be able to contribute money to a specific goal in the *koinōnia* while Christians in a third-world setting may be able to contribute presence and labor.

Fifth, the partnership metaphor is consistent with the concern for mutuality prevalent in our time. In fact, theology today persistently searches for understandings of authority and relationship that are less hierarchical, less arbitrary, less exclusive, and less external than in the past and more participatory, more inclusive, and more internal.[26] The *koinōnia* metaphor provides a way to integrate the Christian perception and use of resources into this concern, for it asks us to see that "we, God, and everybody and everything else are caught up in a big *koinonial* web."[27]

Sixth, the tone of the *koinōnia* passages in the Bible is positive. Among the words that are characteristic of these passages are joy, cheerfulness, liberality, giving not of necessity but freely, grace. This is appropriate to the gospel of the One who is pure, unbounded love.

Notes

1. A brief and readable history of development of the notion of stewardship is Douglas John Hall, *The Steward: A Biblical Symbol Come of Age* (New York: Friendship Press, 1982), pp. 30–41. For a case study of the stewardship theme in the history of a North American denomination, see Clark M. Williamson, "Good Stewards of God's Varied Grace: Theological Reflections on Stewardship in the Disciples" *Encounter* 47 (1986), pp. 64–72.

2. Douglas John Hall, *Christian Mission: The Stewardship of Life in the Kingdom of Death* (New York: Friendship Press, 1985).

3. See David G. Buttrick, *Homiletic* (Philadelphia: Fortress Press, 1987), pp. 5–20.

4. I am indebted to Calvin L. Porter for the basic exegetical insight of this chapter and to Clark M. Williamson, "Good Stewards," pp. 72ff., for theological guidance.

5. T. M. Dorman, "Steward," *The International Standard Bible Encyclopedia*, ed. Geoffrey W. Bromiley et al. (Grand Rapids:

Wm. B. Eerdmans Publishing Co., 1988), vol. 4, pp. 617–618;
C. U. Wolf, "Steward, Stewardship," *The Interpreter's Dictionary of the Bible,* ed. George A. Buttrick et al. (Nashville: Abingdon Press, 1962), vol. 4, p. 443. See Gen. 15:2; 44:4; 1 Chron. 28:1.

6. See 1 Kings 4:6; 16:9; 18:3; 2 Kings 18:18, 37; 19:2; 1 Chron. 29:6; Isa. 36:3, 22; 37:2; Est. 1:8; 8:9.

7. Isa. 22:15–25, esp. 19 and 21.

8. See 1 Kings 9:19; 2 Kings 20:13; Isa. 39:2; Jer. 51:28. God is described as having an *oikonomia* in Psalms 103:22; 114:2; 145:13.

9. Uses of landowner-steward relationship comparable to those of the early Christian writings are also found in the literature of the rabbis. See Otto Michel, *"Oikonomos, Oikonomia," Theological Dictionary of the New Testament,* ed. Gerhard Kittel, trans. Geoffrey W. Bromiley (Grand Rapids: Wm. B. Eerdmans Publishing Co., 1967), vol. 5, p. 149.

10. The word "steward" *(oikonomos)* does not occur in Matthew 25:14–30, but the parallel between the "servants" *(douloi)* in the parable and the role of the steward is quite clear. Furthermore, an *oikonomos* could be a *doulos.*

11. Note, however, that despite the use of the absentee landowner motif in the parables, both Matthew and Luke are clear that God is constantly present in the world (e.g., Matt. 1:23; 18:20; 28:20; Luke 24:5; 24:35; Acts 2:17–20).

12. In actual stewardship sermons, of course, preachers seldom discuss Christian stewardship in the stark manner in which that image is evaluated here. In fact, some preachers and writers seem to distance themselves from weaknesses in the stewardship model even while retaining the vocabulary of the stewardship image and attempting to infuse that vocabulary with meaning which is more appropriate to the gospel. See the writings of Douglas John Hall: *The Steward: A Biblical Symbol Come of Age; Christian Mission: The Stewardship of Life in the Kingdom of Death;* and *Imaging God: Dominion as Stewardship* (Grand Rapids: Wm. B. Eerdmans Publishing Co., 1986).

13. This is clear in the standard studies of *koinōnia* in the Hellenistic age, e.g., H. G. Liddell and Robert Scott, *A Greek-English Lexicon* (Oxford: Clarendon Press, 1968), pp. 968–970; Walter Bauer, W. F. Arndt, F. W. Gingrich, F. W. Danker, *A*

Greek-English Lexicon of the New Testament and Other Early Christian Literature (Chicago: University of Chicago Press, 1979), pp. 438–440; James H. Moulton and George Milligan, *The Vocabulary of the Greek New Testament* (London: Hodder & Stoughton, 1930), pp. 350–351; Friedrich Hauck, *"Koinōnos,"* *Theological Dictionary of the New Testament,* ed. Gerhard Kittel, trans. Geoffrey W. Bromiley (Grand Rapids: Wm. B. Eerdmans Publishing Co., 1965), vol. 3, pp. 789–809, esp. 797–804; J. Y. Campbell, *"Koinōnia* and Its Cognates in the New Testament," *Journal of Biblical Literature* 51 (1932), pp. 352–380; Michael McDermott, "The Biblical Doctrine of *Koinōnia,"* *Biblische Zeitschrift* 19 (1975), pp. 64–78, esp. 65–69, and pp. 219–233; Schuyler Brown, *"Koinōnia* as the Basis of New Testament Ecclesiology?" *One in Christ* 12 (1976), pp. 157–167; M. Jack Suggs, *"Koinōnia* in the New Testament," *Midstream* 23 (1984), pp. 351–362. For different perspectives, see J. G. Davies, *Members One of Another: Aspects of Koinonia* (London: A. R. Mowbray & Co., 1958); George Panikulam, *Koinonia in the New Testament, Analecta Biblica* 85 (Rome: Biblical Institute Press, 1979); Josef Haenz, *Koinonia: "Kirche" als Gemeinschaft bei Paulus*, Biblische Untersuchungen (Regensburg: Friedrich Pustet, 1982).

14. J. Paul Sampley, *Pauline Partnership in Christ* (Philadelphia: Fortress Press, 1980), p. 12.

15. Ibid.

16. Ibid., p. 14.

17. Ibid., p. 15.

18. Ibid., p. 17.

19. Ibid., pp. 25ff.

20. The bibliography on the collection is vast. For representative treatments, see Sampley, *Pauline Partnership*, pp. 82ff.; Keith Nickle, *The Collection,* Studies in Biblical Theology No. 48 (Naperville, Ill.: Alec R. Allenson, 1966); Nils A. Dahl, *Studies in Paul* (Minneapolis: Augsburg Publishing House, 1977), pp. 23–39; H. D. Betz, *2 Corinthians 8 and 9,* Hermeneia (Philadelphia: Fortress Press, 1985); Ernest Best, *Paul and His Converts* (Edinburgh: T. & T. Clark, 1988), pp. 97–106.

21. Sampley does not regard this passage and the next as examples of *koinōnia* in the technical sense of voluntary association.

22. Sampley, *Pauline Partnership,* pp. 62ff.

23. Ibid., p. 58.

24. Ibid., pp. 79–81.

25. Williamson, "Good Stewards," pp. 79–80.

26. See, for example, the writings of Letty M. Russell: *Human Liberation in a Feminist Perspective—A Theology* (Philadelphia: Westminster Press, 1974); *Growth in Partnership* (Philadelphia: Westminster Press, 1981); *Household of Freedom: Authority in Feminist Theology* (Philadelphia: Westminster Press, 1987).

27. Williamson, "Good Stewards," p. 77.

9

Preaching About Giving Thanks— Giving God Thanks and Praise

Fred B. Craddock

Thanksgiving Day provides the occasion for a happy union of Christ and culture. Even those of us who are most diligent to guard against all forms of cultural captivity of the gospel, are willing to call a one-day truce to permit Christ and culture to sit together at the festive table. To be sure, there are those in both pulpit and pew who have taken the unalterable position of setting Christ over against culture, those who refuse, even for a single hour, to leave their posts. For these, more than a principle or a conviction is at stake; rather, it is a matter of identity, for the gospel, they say, is defined in part by what it opposes. To be faithful to the gospel is to rise from the breakfast table every morning to spend the day in combat with Herod. And to be honest, such a posture is not without its reasons. Reflect on what culture has done to Hallows Eve, Christmas, and Easter. Recall how frequently culture breaks into the room where the church keeps its vocabulary, running off with treasured words such as charismatic, grace, love, and even our beloved charity, only to leave them abandoned on the street, used, overused, and misused. And who among us has not been repelled by Thanksgiving festivities in which Uncle Sam and not the Creator was praised, when sheer abundance was celebrated with no thought, no twinge of guilt, no resolve to act relative to the inexcusable gulf between Lazarus and those who fare sumptuously every day? Yes, even Thanksgiving, with all its warmth and joy, has a shadow side and can seduce the unwary.

Even so, most of the faithful come down from the wall, sheathe the sword, and join the larger society on this holiday, which is as much "theirs" as "ours." The realms of creation and redemption enjoy their overlap. The nation pauses to remember benefits forgotten. Families get together as at no other time of year. Airports and highways are more crowded than at Christmas, everyone bent on going home. Churches discard the competitive spirit and join in ecumenical services of praise. The people of the street are invited to banquet tables, and the more reflective among both rich and poor tarry after the meal to get some distance from things, to lament relationships neglected, and to make quiet vows of adjusted priorities. Our hearts agree, "It is meet (fitting) and right to give God thanks and praise."

However, when an act such as giving thanks or a quality such as gratitude is so widely applauded and universally embraced, some of us grow nervous. It is not simply a case of being unable to celebrate the positive or enjoy the triumph of a good. Rather, our uneasiness is due to the sense that unanimous approval of a value tends to blur the distinctive features of that value, to permit it to soften into a vague sentiment, to slip slowly from the list of convictions to the pile of assumptions. The words and music of gratitude left unattended can become for both church and society only a tune hummed now and then, here and there, a tune everyone knows and yet no one knows. What is gratitude anyway? What is it to be thankful? The comments below are intended to offer to the minister suggestions along two lines: (1) explorations into the meaning of gratitude as a quality of character, a virtue, a grace; and (2) occasions in the life of the church on which giving thanks can well be the central thought and act.

Perhaps it should be said at the outset that gratitude is not a quality that submits totally to examination. There is a depth, a complexity, a mystery about thankfulness that remains after even a careful investigation. In both experience and observation we know this to be true. One does not become grateful by an act of will, nor does one seem able to create the quality in others. Persistent and repeated instructions by parents have not guaranteed grateful children. Preachers exhort gratitude and all agree, we ought to be grateful, but. . . . We cannot recall how many times we have shown up for union Thanksgiving services only to find that we were not going to get a glimpse of our inheritance as children of God, we were not going to be permitted to run our fingers through the unsearchable riches of God's grace. Rather, we were excoriated for our ingratitude: "Were not ten cleansed? Where are the nine?" (Luke 17:17). Apparently it is easier to chasten ingratitude than to generate gratitude. Certainly thankfulness has no direct correlation to abundance or to want. Prayers of thanks are said over bread and water while feasts are consumed in arrogant indulgence. And vice versa: the banquet is received in gratitude while the crust of bread is swallowed in bitterness. One traditional mealtime prayer asks, "Lord, make us grateful for this and all your bounty." "Make us grateful": perhaps that is the heart of the matter; God provides not only the food but also the grateful heart. If so, then gratitude is a grace in the true sense of that word. A sketch of biblical terms providing us with the cluster of words such as thankful, thanksgiving, grateful, and gratitude should confirm or correct such a conclusion.

The Roots of the Matter

The central word in a number of related New Testament terms translated "to give thanks" is a Greek verb transliterated *eucharisteō*. From this verb comes one historic term for the Lord's Supper, Eucharist, so named because of the formula, "and when he had given thanks" (1 Cor. 11:24; Mark 14:23). So central was the thanksgiving to the church's understanding and observance of the meal that Eucharist had become a name for the Lord's Supper early in the second century (*Didache* 9). The root from which the word "eucharist" is derived is *charis*, most often but not always translated "grace." Closely related are "charisma," gift, and "charismatic," one who has received a gift. But we should not move too quickly to find theological meanings for these words and leave behind the affective force and social uses of the basic stem word and its derivatives. *Charis* comes from a verb common in Greek culture meaning "to delight, to charm, to give pleasure, to favor, to cause to rejoice," a verb that easily and naturally became a pleasant word of greeting (James 1:1). This force of the term, along with its more theological meaning, can be seen at Acts 11:23, "When he [Barnabas] came and saw the *grace* of God, he was *glad*" (emphasis added). This flavor of the word which, at the hands of New Testament writers, came to have such rich and varied theological and liturgical uses, should not be lost. Thanksgiving is by its very nature joyful, pleasant, and an occasion for delight. Gratitude is not sad, grudging, or mean. Some of this affective force of *charis,* and hence eucharist, is still preserved in our culture in the word "gracious," as in, "Our host was most gracious."

However, when *charis* moved into the web of social and political discourse, it lost some of its freedom and its joy. Such is the sad history of so many great words, a history sometimes chronicled in the New Testament itself. While Luke no doubt wished to retain some of the pleasure in *charis* when he reported that the church in Jerusalem had *"favor* with all the people" (Acts 2:47, emphasis added), he also records the corruption of the word in the hearts and on the lips of those who scheme for advantage. Felix left Paul in prison, "desiring to do the Jews a *favor"* (Acts 24:27, emphasis added), and the same motivation prompted Festus to attempt to return Paul to Jerusalem (Acts 25:9). Only the naïve would miss the political strategy here, such acts of *charis* later becoming IOUs.

This is not to say that *charis* is totally devoid of all expectation from the recipient of the favor or gift. On the contrary, the word may actually refer to a favor shown or a favor received. In other words, *charis,* or "grace," may define an act of giving or an act of receiving: if giving, the word means "gift or unearned favor"; if receiving, then the word is best translated "gratitude." Since the same term represents both sides of the act, it is natural to expect that grace as gift would be met with grace as gratitude. In fact, according to some Greek moralists, gratitude in response to any favor was regarded as a duty and was listed among the ethical qualities. Such reciprocity is not objectionable when it pertains to the normal flow of healthy relationships: giving thanks is a natural and appropriate response to a favor. But in an unhealthy relationship, gifts or favors can be given for the purpose of getting a desired response from the recipient. Such gifts become means of manipulation, actions intended to gain power over another. Favors or apparently gracious acts thus degenerate into a way of saying, "I did you a favor; now you owe me." Such debts are never fully repaid, especially if the benefactions are poisoned by frequent reminders of the debt now due. It is often fear of such manipulation and dehumanizing inevitable in such transactions that causes even the very hungry or the very cold to reject offers of food or clothing. There are conditions worse than being hungry or cold. Recipients who *must* show their gratitude are not free to be truly grateful.

This point is central to the dynamic of thanksgiving. Since *charis* means both gift and gratitude, the freedom of the giving must be matched by freedom in the receiving, else the relationship is diseased. When freedom characterizes the entire dynamic of giving and receiving, both participants experience the beauty and the profundity of "grace." Totally foreign to what takes place is calculating and quantifying. Even if the exercise urged by "Count Your Many Blessings" has some value, it is totally unrelated to our present consideration because of two implications unbecoming to gratitude: (1) that there is a direct correlation between gratitude and the number of one's blessings and (2) that counting blessings will reveal that one is faring better than many others and therefore should prompt gratitude. Comparing one's life with that of persons less fortunate should move one to action but certainly not to gratitude for the difference.

To speak, then, of gratitude is to speak of grace. Even though we began this discussion with the expanded form *eucharisteō* as the principal New Testament word for thanksgiving (Mark 8:6; Matt. 15:36; John 6:11; Acts 27:35; Rom. 16:4; 1 Cor. 1:14; to list but a few examples), we have also seen that the root word *charis,* most often translated "grace," in numerous texts is best translated "thanks." The familiar Pauline formula "thanks be to God" makes use of *charis* (Rom. 6:17; 7:25; 1 Cor. 15:57; 2 Cor. 8:16). Perhaps Paul wants to remind himself that his gratitude is made possible by God's grace.

Grace given by God flows back to God. Notice Paul's double use of the word at 2 Corinthians 9:14–15: "They long for you and pray for you, because of the surpassing *grace* of God in you. *Thanks* be to God for his inexpressible gift!" (emphasis added). So understood, grace prompts gratitude which expresses itself in generosity toward others (2 Cor. 8:1; 9:8) while informing, infusing, and guiding all other Christian qualities, all of them flowing together in praise of God. In fact, Paul understands the basic posture of the Christian to be that of giving thanks, whether one eats or abstains (Rom. 14:6), and he characterizes those alienated from God and darkened in their minds as persons who do not give thanks to God (Rom. 1:21). If one is making a request of God, let it be done with thanksgiving (Phil. 4:6). If one is engaged in witnessing to resistant outsiders, let it be done with thanksgiving (Col. 4:6). If one is watching and waiting expectantly for the Lord's return, then do so with thanksgiving (v. 2). In sum, says Paul, "Give thanks in all circumstances" (1 Thess. 5:18).

This does not mean that negative feelings are to be suppressed or pain and death denied. What it does mean is that the grace of God to which we respond in gratitude is broader, deeper, and more mysterious than any spontaneous good feeling we may enjoy on any given day. The point is, we are not tossing words of gratitude into empty space, nor are we "thanking our lucky stars"; we are thanking God. Gratitude to God is attuned to the attributes of God as creator, sustainer, and redeemer. Thanksgiving searches after God to know God, even while confessing inability to penetrate the thick cloud of God's glory. The believer, often baffled by the weals and woes of the human community and of the whole created order, still stands before the mystery in gratitude, for "from God and through God and to God are all things. To God be glory for ever. Amen" (Rom. 11:36).

The discussion thus far has been in the service of the first suggestion to the preacher: Explore with the congregation the meaning of thanksgiving. This can be done in a single message or it may be sprinkled appropriately through a number of sermons in which giving thanks would be one but not the only line of thought. The avenue taken here has been to explore the single root word in the richly nuanced Greek language that expresses joy, grace, and gratitude, the word early Christians used to convey the essence of the gospel and the believer's response to it. But this is by no means the only way to explore the act of giving thanks. One could as easily turn to the Old Testament and examine ways in which the believer in Israel understood thanking God to be blessing God and to be praising God. In fact, in the comments below we will look at some extraordinary texts in the Old Testament that prompted a saying among the rabbis: "In the future all sacrifices will cease, but the offering of thanks will not cease to all eternity."

Preaching on Occasions of Thanksgiving

We turn now to the second suggestion, which pertains to occasions when the giving of thanks is central not only in the entire service of worship but also in the sermon in particular. Appropriate texts are abundant but attention will be called to only a few among them.

It is true but not sufficient to say that the giving of thanks is fitting at all times and in all places. Such general truths tend in practice to become at no time and nowhere unless we are aided by specific occasions of thanksgiving. And such occasions often call for messages that inform, encourage, and inspire expressions of gratitude. The following selections of occasions and texts are offered as but hints and promptings to those responsible for those messages.

The annual Thanksgiving Day (or Eve) service. In many communities this service is ecumenical, without a fixed tradition of time, place, liturgy, and participants. However, certain features are not optional: the purpose is to express thanks, not to complain about widespread ingratitude; the service is a single act of worship, not a collage of offerings from participating congregations and ministers; and thanksgiving is offered to God, not vaguely nondirectional in case there is someone present who does not believe in God. The message in this service (whether or not it is ecumenical) may be one of two general types. One type is that of recital in which the preacher recalls the great acts of God which prompt the thanksgiving of the community. Such messages are not marked by exegetical detail but by broad affirmations of the power, goodness, and grace of God. Psalm 107 is especially appropriate for such a sermon. It is a psalm of thanksgiving of several stanzas, each including a repeated call for response. All kinds of conditions of human distress are imaged: lost in the desert, in prison, deathly ill, caught in a storm at sea, and oppressed by the powerful. In each case appeal is made to God, the distressed are rescued, and the narrator calls for a response of thanksgiving. With but little elaboration at each stanza the listeners will identify their own past or present experiences and give thanks to God. Psalm 136 is also a psalm of thanksgiving containing a recital of God's activity and a refrain praising God's steadfast love which endures forever. The recital is in three parts: creation, history, and personal life. So sweeping are the stanzas that the preacher can bring into each references from the knowledge and experience of the listeners so as to evoke gratitude and confirmation of the narrator's claim that God's love is steadfast and enduring.

A second type of Thanksgiving Day sermon involves the exposition of a particular text having to do with giving thanks. Here one may be exploring more carefully the sources, the nature, the forms of gratitude. The discussion in the first section of this chapter is similar to what might be done here. Consider, for example, Philippians 4:10–20. Most commentators agree this is a note of thanks from Paul to the church at Philippi, a note that may have originally been sent prior to the letter itself. Look at it as literature: It opens with a joy formula and closes with a doxology. It is filled with language from nature, from business, and from the liturgy of the church. It is obvious that Paul is grateful, but why does he not say so? He is both warm and detached, intimate and distant. He insists he did not need the gift and yet is glad they sent it. This text provides an opportunity to examine the difficulty in saying thanks and to explore the fragility, the depth, the beauty, and the meaning of a seemingly simple act of giving and receiving a gift.

The celebration of the Lord's Supper. Here the texts are firmly set in the tradition: Matt. 26:26–29; Mark 14:22–25; Luke 22:-15–20; 1 Cor. 11:23–26, to which may be added Luke 24:13–35 and John 6:25–59. The meanings are beyond a lifetime of explorations: here is a table of food and drink; here is participation in the body and blood of Christ; here is fellowship in shared bread; here the Passover is recalled, the covenant renewed, and the Parousia anticipated. But strikingly, the church since the second century has given strong attention to the celebration as Eucharist, thanksgiving. All the biblical traditions of the meal include the thanksgiving formula. In John's record of the feeding of the multitude, which is clearly a eucharistic meal, the location of the feeding is referred to as the place of the thanksgiving (John 6:23). For what was Jesus grateful on the eve of his own passion? Why has the church judged thanksgiving to be the heart of the sacrament, so much so that eucharistic prayers became great thanksgivings, recitals of the gracious acts of God? To reflect on this central meaning of the Table is appropriate not only to Communion meditations but also to the pulpit and full sermons which point to the table of thanksgiving.

Fellowship meals. In some congregations, fellowship meals are hurried affairs, serving as incentive to good attendance at choir practice and committee meetings which follow immediately thereafter. No one is of a mind to hear a sermon. However, there are fellowship meals that are meals and they are for fellowship. Such an occasion would be most appropriate for a message on giving thanks. The time, place, and purpose would call for informality and brevity but the importance of what was being said and done could actually be enhanced thereby. It is a meal shared by the family of God, over which a prayer of thanks is said. Reflect on the relationship of this table to the table in the sanctuary, how this meal informs the eucharistic meal and how the Eucharist informs this meal. Could not this fellowship dinner be a eucharistic feast? If so, what would make the transformation? Texts abound that record prayers at meals (Mark 8:1–10; Matt. 15:32–38; Acts 27:33–36). What is most noticeable is that the eucharistic formulas appear here also, as though the Lord's Supper had reinterpreted all meals. In such a message the fellowship hall can be joined to the sanctuary in ways which may have been missed by some of the congregation. Likewise meals in our homes could be united with those at church. Again, one does not want to be too lengthy or require too much work on the part of the listeners, but seriousness of purpose does not require heaviness of manner. For example, one could ask for those in attendance to recall prayers at meals which were learned as children. Or, one might inquire as to whether prayers at the table in our homes are designated as "returning thanks," "asking the blessing" or "saying grace." This could lead to a brief presentation on how grace, gratitude, and blessing are related. As to thanksgiving as blessing God, Psalm 103 would be most helpful. Or one could call attention to the eucharistic formula at Matthew 14:13–21, Mark 6:35–44, and Luke 24:28–35 in which blessing is used instead of thanksgiving. The similarities and differences could also be noted by reading the three prayers (Catholic, Protestant, Jewish) found on cards at the tables in some restaurants. The point is, we often grow in grace by bringing to the conscious level the frequent and familiar, perhaps learning for the first time what we already know.

Occasions of special providence. In every community there are special times when it is good and right to gather in worship and express thanks to God. A long drought ends, flood waters recede, a person ravaged by disease is healed, a missing child is found: at these and countless other times the congregation wants to gather, embrace each other, and thank God. While the service of thanksgiving is prompted by a very present occasion of divine favor, it is important that it not be viewed in isolation but rather be set in the context of the larger story of God's providence. The message can do just that, adding the present event to the recital of God's activity and enrolling the present beneficiaries of divine favor in the larger family of God. Psalm 107, discussed above, would be an excellent text for such an occasion. A beautiful text for a service of thanksgiving for recovery from grave illness is Isaiah 38:9–20, although the message of this text could properly extend to any deliverance from crisis. This passage is also a psalm, "a writing of Hezekiah king of Judah, after he had been sick and had recovered from his sickness" (v. 9). Hezekiah speaks of his pain and the strain put on his relation to God. He calls on God for restoration and in his recovery he begins to see some redeeming value in the illness. In unrestrained gratitude, he vows to witness to God's faithfulness and to sing God's praise in the house of the Lord. Whether the occasion for thanksgiving be restored health, a broken drought, or a found child, the appropriateness of this text lies in its movement from depression and doubt to thanksgiving and praise.

A series of sermons with a common theme. This suggestion does not focus on any particular occasion but on a format for preaching which many ministers and congregations find helpful. Whether or not one follows a lectionary, there are major themes vital to the Christian faith that can be treated helpfully in a series of sermons, the subject matter being of a size too large for a single message. The semicontinuous readings during ordinary time following Pentecost provide the texts for the consideration of some such themes, but not always. If a matter is judged to be of such importance as to warrant a special series, then the preacher might well pursue that judgment. This option is mentioned here because our present subject, giving thanks to God, is of such importance. The preacher who agrees with this assessment might well consider for one such series the thanksgivings that occur at the beginnings of Paul's letters. The thanksgiving was a constituent part of epistolary style prior to Paul and he took it over in his letters to the churches. The thanksgiving follows the salutation (signature, address, greeting) and moves from a personal note to and about the recipients into the subject matter of the letter. In the thanksgiving, personal relationship joins pastoral concerns and theology, all in a spirit of grace and gratitude. Here readers are affirmed and instructed, praised and exhorted, and all this at the altar in thanksgiving before God. All the undisputed letters of Paul open with thanksgivings (or blessings) except for Galatians. That these are all genuine expressions of thanks, full of the substance of the gospel of God's grace, is beyond question; whether they are appropriate for the extended attention of a particular congregation, only the minister of that congregation can judge.

These suggestions are but hints and promptings, touching on times, places, and texts. Behind and beneath all these variables is that which is central and constant: It is fitting and right to give God thanks and praise.

Contributors

Joanna Adams is Pastor of the North Decatur Presbyterian Church in Decatur, Georgia.

Ronald J. Allen is Assistant Professor of Preaching and New Testament at Christian Theological Seminary in Indianapolis, Indiana.

David Buttrick is Professor of Homiletics and Liturgics at the Divinity School of Vanderbilt University in Nashville, Tennessee.

Fred B. Craddock is Professor of Preaching and New Testament at Candler School of Theology in Atlanta, Georgia.

Catherine Gunsalus González is Professor of Church History at Columbia Theological Seminary in Decatur, Georgia.

Richard Lischer is Professor of Homiletics at the Divinity School of Duke University in Durham, North Carolina.

Thomas G. Long is Professor of Preaching and Worship at Princeton Theological Seminary in Princeton, New Jersey.

Neely Dixon McCarter is President of the Pacific School of Religion in Berkeley, California.

Charles L. Rice is Professor of Homiletics at the Theological School of Drew University in Madison, New Jersey.

Don M. Wardlaw is Professor of Preaching and Worship at McCormick Theological Seminary in Chicago, Illinois.